BARK

B A R K

The formation, characteristics, and uses
of bark around the world

• • • • • • • • • • •

photographs by
KJELL B. SANDVED

text by
GHILLEAN TOLMIE PRANCE *and* ANNE E. PRANCE

Published in association with The Royal Botanic Gardens, Kew

TIMBER PRESS
Portland, Oregon

To
Stanwyn G. Shetler,
National Museum of Natural History, Smithsonian Institution,
and
H. C. W. Wilson,
a great teacher of biology

FRONTISPIECE: Flaking, fissured bark covers the swollen trunk of the Queensland
(or narrow-leaved) bottle tree, *Brachychiton rupestris,* from Australia.

ISBN 0-88192-262-5
Printed in Singapore

TIMBER PRESS, INC.
9999 S.W. Wilshire, Suite 124
Portland, Oregon 97225

Library of Congress Cataloging-in-Publication Data

Sandved, Kjell Bloch,
    Bark : the formation, characteristics, and uses of bark around the
world : photographs / by Kjell B. Sandved ; text by Ghillean Tolmie
Prance and Anne E. Prance.
        p.   cm.
    Includes index.
    ISBN 0-88192-262-5
    1. Bark. 2. Bark--Composition. 3. Bark--Utilization. 4. Bark-
-Pictorial works. 5. Photography of bark.   I. Prance, Ghillean T.,
1937-   .   II. Prance, Anne E.   III. Title.
    QK648.S32   1992
    582016'047--dc20   92-19569
                                                              CIP

CONTENTS

ACKNOWLEDGMENTS 6

PREFACE 7

PHOTOGRAPHING BARK 9

INTRODUCTION 13

1 THE STRUCTURE AND FUNCTION OF BARK 23

2 THE FIELD IDENTIFICATION OF BARK 32

3 PHOTOSYNTHETIC BARK 38

4 BARK ECOLOGY 47

5 LATEXES IN BARK 55

6 RESINS IN BARK 62

7 BARK MEDICINES AND POISONS 71

8 HALLUCINOGENIC BARK 78

9 FLAVORS FROM BARK 84

10 BARK TANNINS 90

11 CORK 96

12 BARK CLOTH 103

13 BARK CANOES 116

14 FIBER, FUEL, MULCH, AND OTHER
   USES OF BARK 124

15 BARK AS CAMOUFLAGE AND FOOD 134

16 BARK FLORA 148

17 BARK DWELLERS 162

INDEX OF SCIENTIFIC NAMES 172

GENERAL INDEX 173

ACKNOWLEDGMENTS

We are grateful to the many people who have taught us about bark during the preparation of this book. We thank David Firth of the Peabody Museum, Yale University, for help with the entomological parts; Bobbi Angell for preparing the bark diagrams; Judith Schmidt, Donald Black, David Cutler, David Johnson, and Scott Mori for reading various chapters of this book; Frances Maroncelli and Rosemary Lawlor for typing the different drafts of the chapters; and the library of the New York Botanical Garden for much bibliographic assistance.

GHILLEAN TOLMIE PRANCE
ANNE E. PRANCE

A book of this magnitude would not have been possible without the cooperative efforts of many people during the years it was in progress. Above all, I thank my good friend Barbara Bedette for her encouragement and support during many treks through forests and botanical gardens around the world. I also am grateful to the Director's Office of the National Museum of Natural History, Smithsonian Institution, for the opportunity over the past 32 years to familiarize myself with and to lecture on animal behavior and nature photography for the Smithsonian Educational Programs. I cannot adequately express my gratitude to my many friends at the Smithsonian for their constant encouragement, corrections, and helpful additions, and to the numerous field workers who enabled me to photograph rare specimens in faraway places. Finally, I thank my publishers for their patience and valuable suggestions.

KJELL B. SANDVED

Preface

When I began photographing nature 30 years ago, I had no thoughts of publishing a book on bark. Like my previous nature books, this one simply evolved as one interest opened the door to another.

In 1960 I came to the United States for what I anticipated would be a six-month visit to gather photos for an encyclopedia on animals. I had already published two very successful encyclopedias in Norway on music and art. One of my first stops was at the National Museum of Natural History in Washington, D.C., where I was so captivated by the Smithsonian's vast collections of natural history subjects, its scientific research, and its active educational outreach programs that I soon volunteered to document scientists' research on nature expeditions. I had never taken a photograph before, so I learned the hard way—through hundreds of trials and many errors. Little did I know then that I would not return to Norway or that I would leave a careeer in publishing to become a Smithsonian nature photographer and lecturer.

With the opportunity to observe animal behavior close up, I gradually became aware of how urban creatures take much of nature for granted, often overlooking the "common" things of daily life. A tree trunk, for example, because it often resembles the trunk next to it, captures our imagination about as much as the nearby telephone pole. Compared to a flower, the colorful sexual part of a plant, or compared to a leaf, the symbolic heart and stomach of a plant, bark, the vascular/artery "skin" of a tree, is more prosaic and has always drawn the least attention. Even the Smithsonian's botanical library contains hundreds of books on flowers, a few on leaves, but none with special emphasis on bark.

Despite this lack of attention, bark is remarkably varied and colorful—from the fast-growing rough oak to the slow-growing smooth beech to the scribbly eucalyptus loved by koalas. Thus, while working on books about rain forests, butterflies, orchids, moth behavior, and leaves, I also took extensive photographs of bark from tropical and temperate regions. The more bark examples I photographed, the more I saw how important bark is as a hiding place for insects, as an anchoring area for the roots of orchids and other epiphytic plants, and as a source of various products for the local population.

Throughout my travels I have also been struck by the many native trees and forests which have disappeared from our planet. While filming the excavation of early Bronze Age tombs near the Dead Sea, I noticed a latticework of thousands of undulating horizontal lines on the surrounding hills. Upon closer examination these "lines" turned out to be pebble-strewn, narrow pathways, trodden by foraging goats and camels for ages. The only bark I found along these paths was on low shrubs whose leaves were protected on both surfaces with hard spines. Other, less protected trees had been browsed out of existence through the millennia.

One of the most extensive destructions of trees by the human race has occurred in the Middle East, where forests of beautiful cedars of Lebanon are long gone. As people continue to cut down natural forests at unprecedented rates, they often replace native species with fast-growing commercial trees. Many times these introduced species drastically change the natural ecology of an area. The altered conditions and chemistry of the soil then bring about the irretrievable loss of the area's natural flora and fauna, for with the loss of diverse native plants comes also the loss of animals. This needless destruction of our environment can only be halted and reversed through knowledge, example, and better understanding.

In recent years attitudes toward the environment have changed. The younger generation, in contrast to the hunters of yesteryear, has become a generation of widely informed naturalists who understand the importance of ecological interaction and the consequences of its thoughtless destruction. Leading the way, nature photographers shoot their quarry with a telephoto lens instead of a gun. They have learned that to discover and capture animal behavior on film is a fascinating outdoor sport with all the excitement but none of the finality of shooting to kill. How much greater is the lasting value of a master shot of a living animal, bird, or plant proudly framed on the wall than the stuffed, glassy-eyed head of an animal whose life was abruptly ended.

Many new discoveries await future generations of naturalists. Each discovery, even a small book on the overlooked diversity of bark on trees, lifts the veil and reveals one more side of nature, so close to us, so neglected, and yet so varied and beautiful. Better and more extensive books on bark will no doubt follow this one, but it is my hope that this volume, the first of its kind on bark, will in some small measure act as a catalyst, stimulating the younger generation to train its powers of observation in nature for fun and learning.

KJELL B. SANDVED
National Museum of Natural History
Smithsonian Institution, Washington, D.C.
July, 1992

• • • • • • • • • • •

Photographing Bark

by KJELL B. SANDVED

The diversity of texture, color, and form in bark and its various uses as an anchoring zone for epiphytic plants or as a hiding place for insects and reptiles provide endless sources of delight for nature photographers. Anyone—professionals and amateurs alike—can take good photographs of bark in nature by following a few simple rules.

The most common mistake that causes unsharp, fuzzy pictures is camera shake. No one but the person behind the camera can tell the degree to which he or she shakes, and even then movement is not always noticeable. Needlesharp photographs also depend on the lens and type of film used. To achieve as sharp a picture as your lens and film allow, try the following experiment:

1. Load your camera with 36-exposure slide film, 50 or 64 ASA, preferably Kodachrome or Ektachrome.

2. Crumple a large sheet of aluminum foil and lay it some 20 feet away in ambient light.

3. Using a 50 mm lens, focus on the aluminum foil by turning the lens back and forth over and beyond the sharp area of focus. Then, without hesitation, stop at midpoint and take the picture. Since no one can tell with accuracy when a picture is in sharp focus—only when it goes in or out of focus—this is the best method for focusing.

4. Holding the camera with hands and arms relaxed, expose the film with appropriate lens and diaphragm at 1/2000, 1/1000, 1/750, 1/500, 1/250, 1/125, 1/60, 1/30, 1/15, 1/8, 1/4, 1/2, 1 sec, and 2 sec. Take notes of the exposures.

5. Mount the camera on a tripod and repeat Step 4. Again, be sure to take notes of the exposures.

6. Examine the developed slides against a diffuse light source using a 4× magnifier. If the camera was held steady, the many small reflective sparkles from the aluminum will show as sharp, pinprick stars; if the camera moved, those same sparkles will show as angles, ovals, circles, and so forth.

7. From these important tests you can now determine at which speed you need to expose a scene to get the sharpness you want with your lens and film.

8. Remember, if you change lenses, you must also adjust the length of exposure. For example, if you determine that 1/250 provides the sharpest exposure with your 50 mm lens, when you switch to a 250 mm lens you must decrease the exposure to 1/1000 to get the same sharpness, and when you switch to a 25 mm or a 28 mm wide-angle lens, you must increase the exposure to 1/125.

Often I am asked what is the most challenging decision facing a nature photographer. Is it camera choice? Hardly. I have extensive Nikon equipment, but were I to choose again, I might go with Canon, Minolta, Olympus, Pentax, or some other brand.

Is the type of film the most critical decision? Partly. Kodachrome 25 or 64 ASA is the best film unless a color print is wanted, and then Kodacolor negative film gives superior color. Fuji film is also excellent.

Are lenses important? Yes, to a certain extent. A micro lens with a 1:1 compatibility is excellent for close-up shots, as is a 35–80 mm zoom lens. For greater magnification I reverse the lens on a bellows or, for the ultimate in sharpness in micro-pictures, I use a Zeiss Luminar macro lens, which I have adapted with a double release cable for shooting handheld in the field with electronic flash.

Do self-focusing, auto-exposure cameras guarantee sharp pictures? Yes and no. The common trap that many buyers of new equipment fall into is the belief that superior photographs flow automatically from superior equipment. This is not true. The most impor-

tant element in photography is the person behind the camera; then come a steady hand and good technique.

The photographer is locked into the laws of optics, which are superficially rather simple. The better these laws are understood, the easier it is for the person behind the camera to follow them or to break, bend, and modify them to suit a special purpose. In portrait photography, for example, the way a photographer applies lighting contributes essentially to bringing out the character of the person being photographed and to establishing a mood. The same principle works when photographing bark: the appropriate use of natural and artificial lighting brings out the seemingly simple design elements in bark and creates a certain image.

To learn how light influences an image, observe various small objects intermittently under changing light conditions: front lit, top lit, side lit, back lit, harshly lit by clear noon sun, softly lit under diffused clouds, under polarized light, and with different backgrounds. This exercise teaches the art of visualizing: seeing with the mind's eye. Once the photographer can visualize how the character and color of a close-up scene in nature change with the light, he or she will eventually be able to separate the visual impact of the various design elements from the surrounding background to create a desired image.

To illustrate the simple but important point that angle of light infuences image, take a black pen into a darkened room where a single bare bulb shines. Standing as far away from the light as possible, turn the pen slowly at different angles to the light and notice how a reflective white line appears only at certain angles to the light source. This is precisely what happens in the ridges of certain types of bark when the light hits them at various angles: the image changes with the angle of incoming light. The same principle also explains why a photograph of a spider web taken in clear sunlight or with an electronic flash may hardly turn out unless the photographer diffuses the light or changes the angle. By carefully considering the various effects light has on image, the photographer can use light to highlight the unique design elements in bark.

The visually most prominent design elements in bark, as in all nature, are line, form, texture, color, and space. The importance of each element varies with the amount of emphasis the photographer puts on it.

Lines are by far the most characteristic and varied design features and often the least appreciated. No other design element

OPPOSITE PAGE: Photographer Kjell B. Sandved at work near Belém, Brazil, capturing a strangling fig (*Ficus* sp.) on film.

PHOTOGRAPHING BARK

imparts a stronger attention-compelling, mood-setting influence. Commonly we find curved outlines, straight liines, transitional diagonal lines, finely reticulated lines, and zigzag, radial, or spiral lines. Each type of line creates a certain mood and thus demands a certain lighting. For example, a semicircularly curved object, such as a Roman arch, has an equal change in direction that imparts solidity to the object but may also make it a visual bore. On the other hand, a parabolically or logarithmically curved object, such as a Gothic curve, has unequal change in direction that imparts elegance or lofty exultation to the object. Lines in nature can be subtle or dominant; some impressionists even go so far as to claim that lines do not exist in nature.

Form is a second design element in bark. The photographic rendition of the sculptured form or shape of an object is utterly dependent on the angle and diffusion of the incoming light. Direct light, whether from artificial or natural sources, imparts harshness and contrast to any form. Conversely, a wide light source, such as a large reflector, a diffuser, or a light overcast sky, imparts softness and roundness to a shape. To avoid excessive constrast and hard shadows in bark photographs, a diffuser must be used with harsh light sources. For example, in sunlight from a clear sky that has no diffusing clouds, place a thin sheet of plastic between the sun and the bark to soften the shadows and bring out the bark's texture and form. Similarly, soften light from an electronic flash with a diffuser or use a white umbrella that broadens and diffuses light.

Diffused light gives excellent results in close-up shots, which have the added advantage of allowing the photographer greater control over the direction of incoming light: front, top, side, or back. Front light yields a maximum of color saturation but eliminates the sculptured form of the bark. Top or side light does the reverse: it results in a maximum of sculptured form but with less color saturation. Because front light totally eliminates the form as well as any possible texture in bark, it causes an image to become two-dimensional. Therefore, when photographing bark, attach a strobe light directly to the camera but place it well out to the side and use a diffuser to soften the shadows.

Texture, a third design element in bark, is not only visual but also tactile; that is, people perceive texture both by sight and by touch. The photographic rendition of bark's texture has an even greater critical dependence on the angle of the incoming light than does its form. However, texture is less dependent on the size of the light source than is form. In this way, texture and form are actually interrelated extremes of the same visual perception; texture is in the micro dimension what sculptured form is in the macro. Both are utterly dependent on side or top light and, to a lesser degree, on the size of the light source.

Like texture, the color of bark may vary with the angle of the sun in which it is viewed, the time of day, and the weather conditions. In rain or snow, for example, corklike bark may assume a monotone dark gray aspect. Bark color varies, in part, because the color component of daylight, measured in Kelvin temperature, varies drastically. Under hazy or cloudy weather conditions, the earliest morning sun or late sunset may have an excessive amount of the longer red wavelengths and an absence of the bluer/cyan wavelengths (Kelvin color temperature 2000 to 3000). Thus, green leaves and blue flowers look dark gray while reddish brown objects look much redder. On the other hand, in fog, rain, snow, heavy overcast conditions, or shade, an object illuminated by the blue sky may have an excessive amount of shorter blue wavelengths and an absence of red wavelengths (Kelvin color temperature 8000 to 12,000). Under these conditions, bark assumes a dark cyan tinge.

Color-correcting filters in the strength of CC 10R (red), CC 10Y (yellow), CC 10G (green), CC10C (cyan), CC10B (blue), and CC 10M (magenta) can to a large degree compensate for some of the normally occurring daytime color shifts. Distant forest scenes, for example, will be improved with a UV filter or a haze filter and with a CC 10G (green) color-compensating filter. Reasonably priced, these filters (never touch the surface, only the rim) can be placed loosely in front of the lens behind the protective glass ultraviolet or haze filter.

Some lights—from florescent and incandescent lamps, from a sunset, or even from rain—need stronger filter compensation than do other lights. In general, the setting sun is the least appropriate light source as the reddish glow from the sun's color temperature (Kelvin color temperature 2000) overemphasizes the red. A color-correcting filter in the strength of CC 40C (cyan) can only partially correct for the near-absent cyan color. At other times a photographer may actually use indoor film in the red light of sunrise and sunset.

The last important design element, space, is defined as the area surrounding the tree—in particular, the background—which creates a third dimension to the picture. The choice of background and its treatment greatly affects the visual impact of the tree. When a sharp focus is wanted for the surrounding background, a closed-down normal or wide-angle lens is used to create an illusion of space, although it also adds a perspective distortion. When isolating the tree from its background, a large-aperture normal lens or a moderate telephoto lens is used to compress the image by creating a narrow field of focus or sharpness.

These five design elements, singly or combined, constitute the science of feeling. Using them with forethought, anyone can learn to take good pictures of bark.

How I miss not having another 50 years in which to film the majestic branching growth and lateral expansion of trees! If it were possible to make a time-lapse movie of the growth of a tree by shooting one movie frame every daylight hour for 50 years, we would get roughly a ten-minute movie. What seasonal patterns and textures, what beautiful colors and designs would be revealed to us in the ever-changing bark?

Introduction

The word *bark* brings to mind the sound that a dog makes. For those more botanically inclined, the word may suggest a rather dull, plainly colored, outer covering for tree trunks and branches. This covering, which is more obvious in winter when a tree has lost its leaves, is varied and attractive, often subtly beautiful. It has been found useful in numerous ways.

The many photographs by Kjell Sandved in this book demonstrate the diversity of pattern, color, and texture found in bark. This variety has not come about by chance. It is the result of the long evolutionary history of trees. As trees have adapted to dissimilar environmental conditions, so too bark, the outer protective coat of the tree, has adapted to protect the tree from different elements. When there is danger of fire in the environment, a thick, fire-resistant bark is an obvious advantage. Latex or poisonous chemical compounds are beneficial in bark that is in danger of insect attack. Thus, the varied conditions under which trees grow have led to the evolution of an amazing variety of bark.

The variety in pattern, color, and texture of bark has enabled people to use it in many ways. A native of Amazonia may make a canoe from bark while a Western suburbanite may use bark as a mulch in a garden. Bark has been used for medicines and flavors since ancient times. How flat eggnog would be without a trace of flavor from cinnamon bark, and what sparkle would be missing from some celebrations if there were no champagne corks to pop. Bark has produced rope and cords for clothing, and canvas for bark paintings. Also among its useful products are the tannins used to convert hide into leather for shoes.

In this book we shall explore the many uses of bark. We shall also see how plants, insects, and animals have found numerous uses for bark. Far from being a dull covering for tree trunks and branches, bark is a fascinating and beautiful part of nature as well as an influential part of our lives. Although most people are usually more aware of the uses of trees in their lives and the beauty of flowers, leaves, and fruit, we hope this book will increase awareness of bark, its beauty and usefulness.

ABOVE: The papery bark of the water birch, *Betula occidentalis*, of western North America, shows conspicuous lenticels but neither peels nor flakes.

OPPOSITE PAGE: The fissured bark of a lemon tree, *Citrus limon*, growing in Aburi Botanic Gardens, Ghana.

INTRODUCTION

ABOVE LEFT: The irregular pattern of the spongy bark of *Melaleuca quinquenervia*, the paperbark or tea tree, from Papua, New Guinea.

ABOVE CENTER: The rough bark of *Agathis dammara,* the Amboina pine, from Ambon, Indonesia.

ABOVE RIGHT: The mottled bark of a tree at the Imperial Palace in Kyoto, Japan.

BELOW LEFT: The red flaking bark of a species of *Eucalyptus* from Mount Coot-tha, near Brisbane, Australia.

OPPOSITE PAGE: The old bark of *Eucalyptus pauciflora* subsp. *niphophila.* the snow gum tree, from Mount Ginini, near Canberra, Australia, has a characteristic gray color while the new bark is smooth and white.

INTRODUCTION

ABOVE: The reddish brown scales of the bark of the lemon-scented gum tree, *Eucalyptus citriodora,* contrast with the smooth gray trunk.

BELOW: The colors and patterns on this branch of Queensland pine, *Agathis robusta,* are formed by lichens.

BELOW: The flaking reddish outer bark of the gumbo-limbo tree, *Bursera simaruba,* from Belize, reveals the green living inner bark.

BELOW: The bay berry, *Pimenta acris,* a relation of allspice, has a smooth brown bark that is characteristic of many members of the myrtle family.

INTRODUCTION

OPPOSITE PAGE, LEFT: The corky texture of a vine of *Rhoicissus rhomboidea* from southern Madagascar, is a woody relative of the familiar houseplant kalanchoe.

OPPOSITE PAGE, RIGHT: The velvetleaf or feltbush tree, *Kalanchoe beharensis*. from southern Madagascar, is a woody relative of the familiar houseplant kalanchoe.

ABOVE: The young bark of the saman or monkeypod tree, *Samanea saman,* from the West Indies is covered by conspicuous lenticels.

BELOW: The distinctive texture and pattern on the stem of the dragon tree, *Dracaena ellenbeckiana,* is formed from the scars of the leaf bases. The bark of some species of *Dracaena* yields a red resin, called dragon's blood, which is used to color varnish and in photo-engraving.

OVERLEAF: The smooth gray bark of an old cabbage gum tree, *Eucalyptus pauciflora,* from Mount Ginini, Australia.

• • • • • • • • • • •

CHAPTER 1

The Structure and Function of Bark

The trees of the Lord are full of sap:
even the cedars of Libanus which he planted.

PSALM 104:15

It is often the bark of a tree which gives the tree its characteristic appearance. Some species, such as the shagbark hickory (*Carya ovata*), which looks like a hairy monster, or the London plane (*Platanus × acerifolia*) with its smooth flaking bark, are most distinctive; others have a more generalized bark type.

A casual glance at a piece of bark which has fallen from a burning log in a fireplace shows that bark consists of several layers of different types of tissue. There are technical terms for these layers, but even experts use these terms in different ways. *Bark*, a nontechnical word, has been used to describe only the outermost corky layer of the covering of a tree, or the entire multilayered unit of outer shell that can be easily detached from the wood. In this book we will use the word *bark* in the latter sense, to include all the outer layers of a tree covering.

Surrounding the wood of any tree is a cylinder of cells called the *vascular cambium*. These cells divide and produce new cells which build up the wood on the inside of the cylinder, and the phloem or inner bark on the outside of the cylinder. It is because of this ring of cells that a tree grows laterally, that is, by increasing the trunk diameter.

Zones of plant cells that are capable of dividing to increase the number of cells are termed *meristems*. The vascular cambium, so named because it produces the vascular or nutrient-transporting tissues, is a meristem layer. Bark, then, consists of all the layers of tissue that lie outside this meristem layer. During the spring when the cells of the cambium are actively dividing, it is easy to remove the bark of most temperate-region trees. When the bark is removed, the cambium, which remains attached to the wood, appears as a slimy layer encircling the wood of the trunk or branch.

Bark is composed of two principal zones: the *inner bark*, or bast, and the *outer bark*. The inner bark has the phloem or conductive tissue by which sugars are transported from the leaves in the crown of the tree to the roots, and from storage tissues to other parts of the plant in the spring. While the inner bark, with its food-conducting tissue, is essential to the life of the tree, the primary purpose of the outer bark is to protect the tree.

Let us look first at the outer protective coat of bark, the periderm. It is usually divided into three layers, each one described by a special term formed from the Greek word *phellos*, meaning cork. The outer layer, the phellem, consists of true cork. Next is the phellogen (from *phell* + *gen*, meaning to produce) or cork-producing layer. The innermost layer, the phelloderm, is named from *derma*, the Greek word for skin. Another term for outer bark is *rhytidome*; derived from the Greek word for a wrinkle, rhytidome describes bark's wrinkled appearance. However, since *periderm* is the term used most often for the outer bark, we will not use the word *rhytidome* any more in this volume.

The entire outer bark consists of the periderm layers and frequently old dead phloem from the inner layers. The phellogen, also called the cork cambium, is a meristem which produces cork cells to the outside. These cork cells are usually tightly packed and have fatty substances (waxes and suberin) deposited in their walls. The fatty substances give cork its special property, namely, the ability to restrict the passage of water. Cork cells are typically dead, and their interiors are filled with air. Hence, cork is usually light in weight and provides thermal insulation. Sometimes cork cells are thick-walled and therefore less resilient. They may contain other organic substances, such as tannins or resins which give them color. The cork cambium may also produce greater or lesser amounts of living cells to the inside (the phelloderm).

The outer appearance of a tree depends on the type of cork and phelloderm cells produced (whether thin-walled or thick-walled), on the relative amount of cambial products, and on the amount and type of secondary phloem that is included in this layer. In some cases, the outer bark is made up mostly of secondary phloem fibers and thus has a fibrous texture. An example is the sapucaia nut of Brazil (*Lecythis pisonis*). In other instances, such as the cork oak, the cork cambium is very active and produces a thick layer of cork, while the fiber layer is thin or even absent. Some barks, such as birch, have a papery nature because the phellogen alternately produces several layers of thicker-walled cells followed by several layers of thin-walled cells. The thin-walled cells are fragile, and the thicker layers can separate as sheets.

The outer bark of many trees has small dots or studlike marks called *lenticels*. This term, like most of the scientific terminology for parts of a tree, is derived from a classical language. In this case, *lentis* is Latin for lentil; many of the lenticels are lentil shaped.

Lenticels are pores of the bark. They are openings or small passages through the periderm made of loose cells that have not become completely corky and so leave air spaces between corky cells. Like stomata, the breathing pores of leaves, lenticels are essential for the life of the tree as it is through them that gas exchange can take place. In young trees, they occur usually where the original epidermis of the young stem had stomata.

Lenticels vary in size from species to species. In some species they are microscopic, but in others they are visible to the naked eye and can be up to ⅜ inch (1 centimeter) in diameter. The lenticels in birch and cherry bark are easy to see, as are the lenticel passages in the cork of a wine bottle. The dark brown transverse powdery streaks in cork are the passages of the lenticels which enable the cork oak to breath through its extremely thick protective covering of cork.

The German plant physiologist G. Haberlandt showed in 1914 that blocking the lenticels of certain trees affected their gas exchange and the rate of water loss. Trees need a thick protective coating of bark, but they also need a way to allow gas exchange through the layer of cork.

The second principal zone of bark, the inner bark, is called by three names: the inner bark, the phloem, or the bast. Inner bark is essential to the life and life-support systems of the tree, and as with any important system in a living organism, it is complex in structure and function. It is composed of several types of cells, each of which has a significant role in the life of the tree. Among these are sieve tube elements (which make up sieve tubes), fiber cells, companion cells, parenchyma cells, ideoblasts, and lactifers. Not all cell types occur in every bark. For example, lactifers or latex-bearing cells occur only in trees with latex, the birthwort genus *Aristolochia* has no phloem fibers, and conifers have sieve cells and albuminous cells, but lack the division of labor into sieve tube elements and companion cells.

The inner bark lies between the vascular cambium and the outer cork cambium, that is, between the two layers where cell division and, consequently, growth take place. It is built up from the vascular

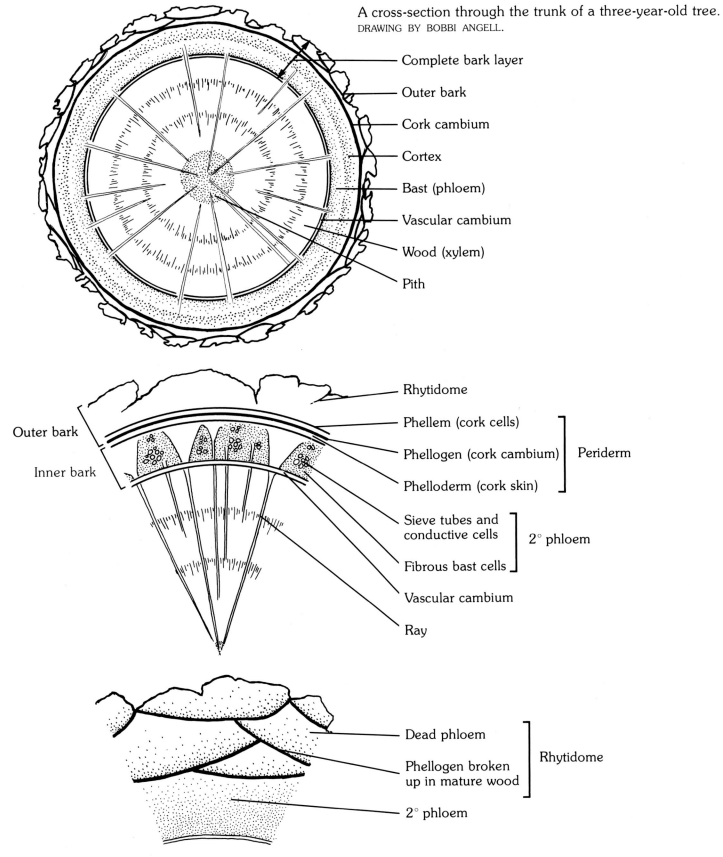

A cross-section through the trunk of a three-year-old tree.
DRAWING BY BOBBI ANGELL.

Complete bark layer

Outer bark

Cork cambium

Cortex

Bast (phloem)

Vascular cambium

Wood (xylem)

Pith

Rhytidome

Outer bark

Inner bark

Phellem (cork cells)

Phellogen (cork cambium) — Periderm

Phelloderm (cork skin)

Sieve tubes and
conductive cells

Fibrous bast cells — 2° phloem

Vascular cambium

Ray

Dead phloem

Phellogen broken
up in mature wood — Rhytidome

2° phloem

cambium. If a tree is not infected by fungus or bacteria, it will continue to live when its outer bark is removed, but the inner bark is part of the tree's life-support system. Foresters apply this principle in ring barking or girdling, a process in which a cylinder of outer and inner bark is removed from a tree. If the ring completely encircles the tree, the tree normally dies because its arteries have been severed. Other exploiters of tree bark, such as the Mediterranean cork-gatherers or the Native American birch bark canoe constructors, are careful to remove only the outer bark to avoid killing the trees upon which their livelihood depends. Fruit growers also use partial girdling of trees to reduce vigor and to induce early fruiting.

Just as the human body has two types of passage for blood circulation, one that carries blood to the heart and another to carry it away, so a tree has separate systems for moving liquids to and from the leaves. Water that is absorbed through the roots and forms the basis for root sap is carried up to the leaves through conductive cells. These cells, called vessels and tracheids, are present in the wood, not in the bark. For this reason it its necessary to drill through the bark and into the wood of a maple tree to tap the sap as it surges to the crown of the tree in spring for the formation of new leaves. When concentrated by boiling down, this maple sap makes maple sugar. Root sap in trees is carried to the leaves because the process of photosynthesis takes place only in the leaves. The resulting products of photosynthesis, mainly sugars, must then flow downwards to the trunk and roots so these parts can continue to grow and function. Unlike the rising sap in the wood, this downward flow is through the conductive tubes of inner bark, called the phloem. As the sap travels to the trunk and roots, some of it is distributed horizontally through the wood by means of ray cells. In this way the entire tree is nourished.

The conducting cells of the phloem through which the nutrients are transported in their downward journey are elongate cells. In conifers and flowering plants, they are called sieve cells or sieve tubes, and are composed of sieve tube elements. These cells look like microscopic sieves with minute pores in the cell walls. The nutrients pass through the sieves from cell to cell.

In addition to conducting cells, inner bark contains fiber, parenchyma cells, and ideoblasts. Fiber cells led to the term *bast*, a word derived from the verb *to bind*. Useful bark fibers such as flax, hemp, and ramie are phloem fiber tissue. Parenchyma cells store starch, fats, and other food materials for the tree. Tannins and resins can also accumulate in them. Ideoblasts secrete a variety of substances, such as balsams, gums, mucilages, oils, resins, and tannins. Another type of cell common in the inner bark is the lactifer, or latex-containing cell. The lactifers of the rubber tree (*Hevea*) are the source of commercial rubber. Thus, it is evident that the inner bark of trees provides the human race with many useful products.

Since the inner bark is vital to the tree, it is not surprising that it is well protected by the thick, corky outer bark, and defended from predators by the presence of resins, latex, tannins, and substances poisonous and noxious to bark-boring insects and fungal diseases.

Bark is not merely a waste product that impedes access to the real wood. It is one of nature's marvels, which provides humans with important products and the tree with protection and an arterial system.

BELOW: The damaged trunk of a Brazilian ironwood tree, *Caesalpinia ferrea*, shows various bark layers. A callus has formed over the inner bark to protect it. The paler reddish area is the periderm.

RIGHT: The trunk of the India rubber tree, *Ficus elastica*, is distinctive because of its horizontal lines of lenticels.

BELOW TOP: The small brown dots on this tree trunk are lenticels or breathing pores of the bark.

BELOW BOTTOM: Lenticels take on different shapes and arrangements, adding to the variety of patterns on tree trunks. This benjamin fig, *Ficus benjamina*, from Java has conspicuous horizontal lenticels.

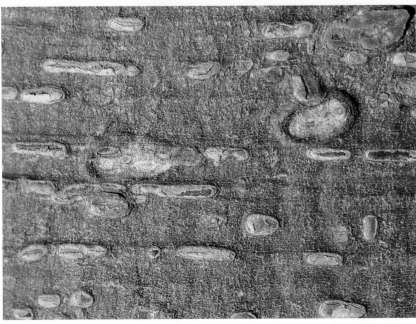

OPPOSITE PAGE: The large lenticels of the earpod or elephant's-ear tree, *Enterolobium cyclocarpum*, can be seen up the trunk.

LEFT: The candle-bark gum tree, *Eucalyptus rubida*, from Canberra, Australia, has a very thin scaly bark that peels off in strips.

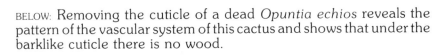

TOP LEFT: The giant prickly pear cactus, *Opuntia echios*, from Galapagos Island, has a barklike outer covering.

BOTTOM LEFT: The Canary Island pine, *Pinus canariensis*, has a thick, fissured, corky bark.

BELOW: Removing the cuticle of a dead *Opuntia echios* reveals the pattern of the vascular system of this cactus and shows that under the barklike cuticle there is no wood.

BELOW LEFT: The inner bark of *Cinnamomum camphora*, the camphor tree, secretes an aromatic oil, which protects the tree from insects. Camphor oil is also used as an insect repellant to protect fabrics from moths and as a stabilizer in the manufacture of certain plastics.

BELOW RIGHT: Many trees in the tropical rain forest depend on a well-developed stilt or prop root system for greater stability in the soft, water-soaked soils and for added water uptake in their highly competitive environment.

• • • • • • • • • • • •

CHAPTER 2

The Field Identification of Bark

Bark is regarded frequently as an obstruction and waste material which must be removed to reach the wood. However, to many field foresters or tree spotters bark is a useful indication of wood quality and tree species.

Often telltale irregularities in the bark inform foresters of similar irregularities in the wood. For example, scars usually remain visible in the bark long after a branch has fallen. These scars not only indicate where the branch was once attached to the tree, but they also indicate the presence of a knot that may penetrate deeply into the wood below. When the scar is a steeply sided swelling with a rough border, the knot is probably shallow, but if the scar is only a small swelling that blends into a smooth border, the knot has sunk deeper into the wood.

Foresters can also use bark features to identify trees. It is obvious in any North American or European forest that each species of tree has a different type of bark. There are some look-alikes, but on the other hand it is easy to recognize the distinct smooth white bark of many birches or the untidy scaling bark of shagbark hickory, and to distinguish an oak from a maple by the bark. In a northern temperate forest, where a limited number of species exist, it may not be as critical to distinguish trees by their bark. However, in a tropical forest, where there is great diversity of tree species, it is essential for foresters to be able to discriminate between them. Characteristic bark can be one of the indicators of a certain species.

In our field work in the Amazon forests of Brazil, we have spent many hours with professional tree spotters. By making a small slash into the bark with a machete, they can usually identify the species of tree. This method is so reliable for experienced field workers that they can make correct identifications even in the species-rich Amazon forest, where a single acre may contain 100 species of trees. Although many species look very similar, some are distinct at first glance; for example, *Couepia elata* has a shaggy bark like hickory, but the mulatta tree (*Calycophyllum*) has an absolutely smooth brown bark that resembles strikingly the brown skin of a mulatto. However, once the 10 easy-to-identify trees have been picked out, 90 others are left in the tropical rainforest study plot.

The bark characteristics which tree spotters in the tropics use to identify trees are numerous. Often they are features which were recognized first by indigenous peoples who later showed them to settlers. Because these characteristics have been known for many years, the local name for a tree often reflects some characteristics of its bark. One such example is *macucu chiador* (*Licania hetero-morpha* Benth.), a common Amazonian tree whose name means hissing macucu. It comes from the Portuguese word *chiar* (to hiss); *Macucu* is the name given for many species of the genus *Licania*. The tree was so named because when its bark is slashed, there is a long hiss from the trunk like the sound of pressurized steam escaping through a small hole. The slash obviously releases air pressure in the phloem of its inner bark.

A relative of *macucu chiador* is called *macucu sangue* (*sangue* = blood) because when slashed, its bark exudes a red sap that looks like blood. Yet another species of the genus *Licania* is called *farinha seca* (dry flour). When slashed, the outer bark of this tree breaks up into little pieces which resemble cassava flour, the staple diet of many Amazonians. *Corythophora rimosa*, a relative of the Brazil nut tree, is called *castanha jacare* or alligator nut. Its deeply fissured bark is reminiscent of an alligator skin. Similarly, one Amazon laurel is called *lauro piraracu* because its bark has scales that look like those of the Amazon's largest scalefish, the giant piraracu (*Arapaima gigas*).

One of the field men with whom we have often worked, Milton da Silva from the Goeldi Natural History Museum in Belém, Brazil, is nicknamed "*Cheira pau*," which means "tree sniffer" in Portuguese. First he makes a bark slash, then he smells a piece of the bark. He can identify many different species of tree by the smell of the phloem alone because of the chemical compounds (such as essential oils) in the living bark. Well-known odors, such as cinnamon bark, are easy to recognize, but the fine distinctions which Milton and many other

tree spotters make are the ultimate test of any olfactory system. How often his field diagnosis based on smell has been proven correct when specimens from the tree have been studied later and identified scientifically.

Subtle distinctions in bark color are also used by tree spotters to distinguish related tree species. The legume tree *Macrolobium limbatum*, for example, has a pinkish hue to its bark slash which distinguishes it from related species. Similarly the Brazil nut relative *mata mata preto* (*Eschweilera odora*) has a bark which is dark in comparison to others in that genus. The characteristic dark bark gives this tree its common name: *mata mata* is the local name for all Brazilian Amazonian *Eschweilera* trees, and *preto* is Portuguese for black. The cupiuba tree (*Goupia glabra*) can be recognized by its very dark bark, and the *ampá doce* (*Brosimum parinarioides*) tree has a pattern of alternating dark and light patches in the outer bark, which make it quite distinctive.

When tree spotters slash the bark, they are alert not only to its color and odor, but also to its consistency. The way in which the machete reacts to the trunk can be a clue in identifying the species. In some trees the machete enters into the bark easily. In others, such as the *Licania* species called *caripe*, the machete makes a ringing sound as it strikes the bark. In the case of the copal treee *Hymenaea courbaril*, or *jatobá* as it is called in the Amazon, the bark is so hard that the machete bounces back rather than entering the bark.

In addition to clues from smell, color, and consistency, tree spotters use clues from texture. Often they pull on a small sliver of bark from the slash to see if it peels down in a strip or breaks off. In fibrous barks the sliver may peel into a long ropelike section. Trees with this kind of fibrous bark are called *envira* in Brazil. Since almost all members of the Annona family (Annonaceae) have fibrous bark, the local name for most of them is *envira*. It is not a definitive characteristic of the Annonas, however, as many other trees in unrelated plant families produce *envira*, including members of the Brazil nut family, especially in the genus *Couratari*, and some members of the cocoa family, Sterculiaceae.

Another useful clue to tree identification is the presence of latex, resin, or a colored sap. The presence of latex, for example, reduces the number of plant families to which a tree could belong by about 60 percent. This number can be further refined by the color or taste of the latex. Members of the fig family tend to have a brown- or cream-colored latex that tastes sweet. Other latex is sour, and in many families, such as the Euphorbiaceae to which rubber (*Hevea*) belongs, it is pure white. A yellow or orange latex indicates the tree may belong to Guttiferae, as most trees in the Amazon forest with yellow and orange latex belong to this family.

It is clear that bark has many characteristics which aid identification. Nonetheless, there are some snags and pitfalls in this method. The first is that many species have similar barks. For example, members of *Humiria* often have barks which closely resemble those of

Licania in the unrelated Chrysobalanaceae. Another difficulty arises from the elusive qualities of smell, sound, and color which are difficult to capture in words. Field notes on the odor of a particular bark or the sound it makes when struck may not evoke the same odor or sound for the scientist studying the tree. However, careful observation of bark can often be of great assistance in identifying a tree, especially when bark information is added to other tree characteristics such as leaf shape and type, forms of the flower and fruit, or even the growth habit of the tree.

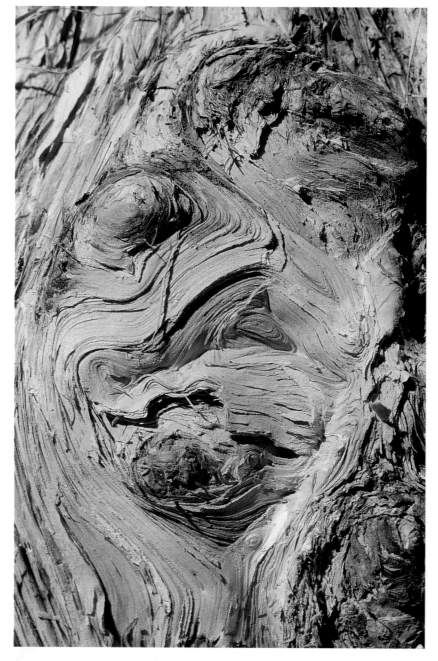

ABOVE: The untidy scaling bark of the shagbark hickory tree, *Carya ovata*, clearly distinguishes the species. Photo © Joyce A. Coleman.

LEFT: The pattern in the bark of this *Melaleuca minor* from Sulawesi, Indonesia, is formed by knots in the wood.

THE FIELD IDENTIFICATION OF BARK

LEFT: Amazonian field workers identify many tree species from their bark characteristics by making a slash in the trunk with a machete. Photo © G. T. Prance.

BELOW LEFT: The unusual patterns on the bark of this *Artocarpus altissima* tree from Sumatra make it easily recognizable in the field.

BELOW RIGHT: This tree from Mount Etinde, Cameroon, has a distinctive yellow latex that is typical of members of the Guttiferae (*Garcinia* family). Photo © G. T. Prance.

THE FIELD IDENTIFICATION OF BARK

BELOW: The wavy bark of this *Eucalyptus* from Canberra, Australia, makes it easy to identify.

BELOW: Once an important source of natural rubber, the India rubber tree, *Ficus elastica,* has a distinctive bark.

The bark of the cacao tree, *Theobroma cacao,* is distinctive in part because of the flowers and fruit that grow directly out of the trunk. Relatively few species share this characteristic called cauliflory. The cacao tree is cultivated throughout lowland tropical America for its seeds, the primary source of cocoa and chocolate.

• • • • • • • • • • • • • • •

CHAPTER 3

Photosynthetic Bark

When we visualize a leaf, we most frequently expect it to be green, but when we visualize bark, green is not the first color we imagine. We expect bark to be some shade of brown, gray, or silvery white. If we look closely at the bark of young twigs on a tree, however, we see they are often green. This greenness indicates the presence of chlorophyll.

Chlorophyll is the green pigment that is an essential agent in photosynthesis, the process by which plants use solar energy to produce sugars and oxygen from carbon dioxide and water. This chemical reaction usually takes place in the leaves, especially in trees of the temperate and humid tropical regions of the world. But nature is always very resourceful, and when a plant has no leaves— a cactus, for example—chlorophyll is found in the stem. Often trees in hot, arid regions have a similar adaptation, and it is these that most frequently have green bark on their trunks.

Trees in these arid regions lose their leaves during the long dry season. Often they have leaves for only two or three months of the year. If they retained their leaves through the dry season, the tree would lose too much water through transpiration, the evaporation of water from the leaves. This is also why desert cacti and many other succulents have no leaves but rely only on the stem for photosynthesis.

Some of the arid region trees are able to maintain a low rate of photosynthesis to keep them alive and active by having a green layer, or chlorenchyma, beneath a very thin cork layer. A well-known example is the *Bursera simaruba*, called gumbo-limbo in Florida and naked Indian tree in the Caribbean and Central America. Its local name comes from its bark which is reddish brown, very smooth, and beautiful. The tree constantly sheds layers of bark in the same way that the birch does in the northern temperate forests. These layers are extremely thin and photosynthetic, their thinness being maintained through the exfoliation process. Underneath the very thin cork is a thick layer of green tissue, rich in chlorophyll.

Unlike other barks, smooth green or brown barks do not have a rhytidome layer of dead cork cells; instead they maintain a periderm throughout their lifetime.

The small tree *Parkinsonia aculeata*, common in the arid zones of the Caribbean and Central and South America, has the local name *palo verde* (green tree) because of its green trunk. Like the naked Indian tree, it maintains a translucent epidermis and a thin photosynthetic bark. Other trees of arid regions with green bark include *Cercidum praecox*, *C. torreyanum*, and various members of the bombax family (Bombacaceae) such as *Pseudobombax maximum* and *Pachira*. In some members of the Bombacaceae, the green areas are only in strips of the bark.

Green bark demonstrates the adaptability of nature. It is one of the ingenious ways by which plants grow in the hostile, dry environment of semideserts (such as the semideserts of northeastern Brazil which are known as Caatingas), and the arid regions of Mexico and northern South America.

The gray bark of the Queensland bottle tree, *Brachychiton rupestris,* is what most people think of as typical-looking bark.

ABOVE: The gum tree, *Eucalyptus deglupta,* is a good example of a tree with green photosynthetic bark. Instead of forming a thick corky layer, the outer bark peels off regularly.

LEFT: The Madagascan *Pachypodium rutenbergianum* tree flowers in a leafless condition showing a green photosynthetic bark.

ABOVE: The freshly exposed green bark of *Eucalyptus deglupta* contrasts with the old, peeling brown layers.

RIGHT: The trunk of *Bursera simaruba*, the gumbo-limbo tree, from Pico Rondon, Brazil, is almost entirely green. Green-barked trees are found more frequently in arid areas, where trees in a leafless condition continue photosynthesis through their bark. Photo © G. T. Prance.

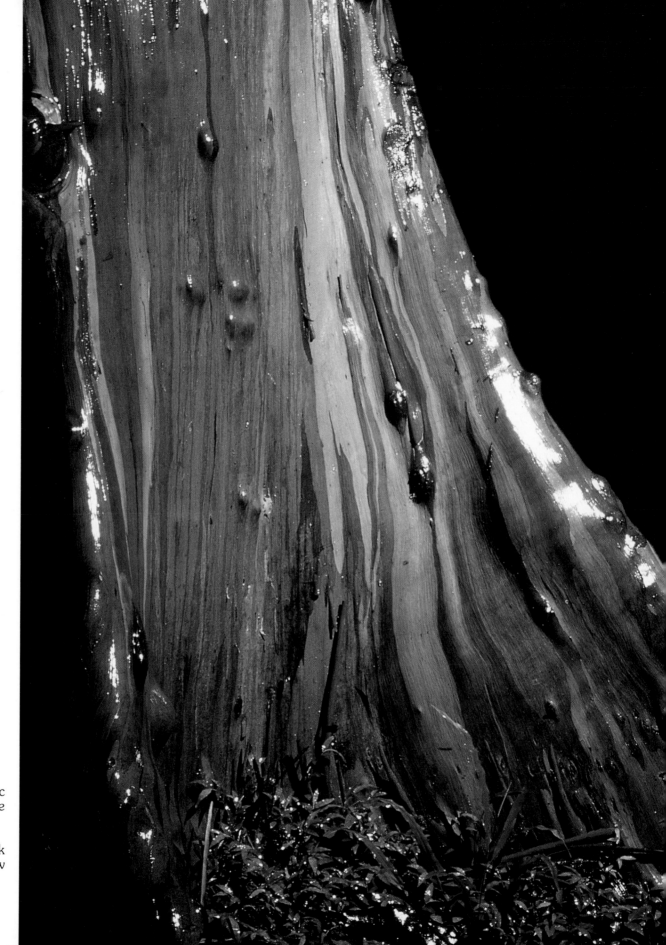

RIGHT: The colorful photosynthetic bark of *Eucalyptus naudiniana*, the silk tree.

OPPOSITE PAGE: Bark patterns on a silk tree, *Eucalyptus naudiniana*, show the successive scaly layers.

PHOTOSYNTHETIC BARK

43

ABOVE: The strawberry tree, *Arbutus unedo,* is a European species with a green inner bark.

ABOVE: Some trees have green photosynthetic bark in cracks, while the rest of the bark is thick and corky. The red silk-cotton tree, *Bombax malabaricum,* from Indochina, shows green photosynthetic bark in the areas between its spines.

ABOVE: The trunk of *Eriodendron anfractuosum,* an African member of the bombax family, has spines and areas of green bark.

TOP RIGHT: The Mexican shaving-brush tree, *Pseudobombax ellipticum,* has green lines all over its gray trunk.

BOTTOM RIGHT: The trunk of *Stereospermum kunthianum,* an African member of the catalpa family, is covered with a colorful mixture of green bark and lichens.

PHOTOSYNTHETIC BARK

The paper-thin scaling bark of *Bursera simaruba*, the gumbo-limbo tree, from Pico Rondon, Brazil. Because of its bark, this tree is also known as the West Indian birch tree. Photo © G. T. Prance.

• • • • • • • • • • • •

CHAPTER 4

Bark Ecology

Lay aside your cloak, O Birch-Tree,
Lay aside your white-skin wrapper.

HENRY LONGFELLOW
The Song of Hiawatha

Bark takes many forms throughout the world. It ranges from the paper-thin, scaling, green photosynthetic bark found on many trees in the arid regions to the extremely thick, corky bark of the cork oak or the redwood trees of California. This variety is not haphazard but, as in other living organisms, is linked to features within a given habitat.

Numerous factors influence the forms that bark takes; among them are the tree's growth pattern, its need for defense against predators, its lack of photosynthetic tissue in the leafless condition, and its need for insulation against either heat or cold. Many of these factors are linked to the ecology of the tree, that is, to the habitat in which it grows. The link is especially clear in an arid area where water conservation is essential to maintain life. There trees remain leafless for up to 10 months, and so the green bark assumes the life-sustaining photosynthetic function usually performed by the leaves.

The link between habitat and type of bark is also evident in other situations; for example, some habitats are more prone to natural fires than others. In the extremely arid, semidesert habitats, where green-barked trees occur most frequently, natural fires are not part of the typical life cycle of the vegetation because usually there is insufficient biomass for the vegetation to catch fire. However, in tropical savannas and the pine and redwood forests of California, natural fires would occur even if these areas were left undisturbed by people.

Natural fires are occasionally caused by falling igneous rock from volcanoes and meteorites, but generally they are caused by lightning striking the tinder-dry vegetation. In the seasonal tropics, for example, a long dry season is often followed by a period of dramatic thunderstorms as the rainy season begins. Under these conditions, the grassland savannas are most likely to catch fire. In fact, it has been estimated that lightning causes about 50,000 vegetation fires annually worldwide. Ten thousand of these occur in the United States, with at least eight thousand occurring in the Rocky Mountain and western regions.

In habitats where natural fires often occur, trees must develop a means of surviving the heat. They frequently achieve this by developing a specialized bark which is thick and corky. It is one of the most noticeable characteristics of tropical savanna trees. Many unrelated species have a thick, grooved bark structure, whereas their closest relatives in other habitats have a thinner bark that is much nearer normal thickness. Those species of trees that are scattered throughout the tropical grasslands have developed a thick, corky bark because cork is a good insulator and does not burn. Fire may scorch the leaves of these species, but the corky bark protects the vital parts of the trees which soon put out new foliage after a fire.

Other trees in tropical savannas have adapted to fire by going underground. These species, called suffruteces, have underground trunks and branches that spread over a large area and put up only small branches above the ground; an example is the rhea fruit, *Parinari obtusifolia,* from the savannas of central Brazil. When a fire occurs, the leaf-bearing shoots are burnt, but the tree sprouts again from its underground trunk and branches. Suffruteces do not need to protect their trunks and branches with corky bark as the earth provides them with insulation.

Natural fires also occur regularly in many forests of the western United States. In dry ponderosa pine forests, for example, it is estimated that natural fires occur on an average of once every 6 to 7 years, and very few areas go for more than 18 years without a fire.

These fires eliminate the undergrowth and so enhance the growing conditions for many species of trees. A fear of forest fires has mistakenly led people to prevent them in areas naturally adapted to fire, such as the redwood forests, but just as trees in tropical savannas have thick, fire-resistant bark, some of the thickest barked trees in North America are species that grow in habitats prone to fire. Such familiar trees as the Douglas fir, red pine, western larch, giant sequoia, redwood, and many species of oaks and pines have a thick insulating bark which has evolved because of the frequent fires in their natural habitat.

In 1930 forester Howard Flint published a study of the use of fire in the management of the national forests of northern Idaho. He determined the relative resistance to fire of the major species in this northern Rocky Mountain area. Measuring such features as bark thickness, rooting habit, and resin content of the old bark and correlating these data with survival after fire, he found that all the trees classified as very resistant to fire had a thick bark. Included among them were the western larch, the ponderosa pine, and the Douglas fir.

Not all bark is fire resistant. In contrast to corky, fire-resistant bark, in some other habitats bark can be quite flammable. For example, the barks of birch and some species growing in areas where fire is a regular part of the natural life cycle have developed an insulative, protective layer of bark.

Another feature of bark that is linked to the ecology of a tree is the occurrence of large spines in the trunk of the tree. The young trunk of the kapok or silk-cotton tree of the tropics is an example. A large number of trees have pure cork prickles which arise in the phellogen of the bark and grow outward as a ferocious protection for the tree. Many woody members of the rue family, Rutaceae, have the prickles, such as the espino tree (*Zanthoxylum martinicense*), common in the forests of several Caribbean islands. Another large tree of the South American forest, the sandbox tree (*Hura crepitans*), is quite impossible to climb because of its spinous trunk. These cork prickles tend to occur most on trees that grow in areas where there is the need of protection from predators. Large browsing animals will avoid trunks that are fortified with spines. Some of these adaptations may have evolved in defense against large animals which have long gone extinct.

Because bark is a functional and vital part of a tree, it is often varied in texture, thickness, and type according to the hostile features of the environment in which the tree grows.

ABOVE: Tropical savanna trees, such as *Antonia ovata* from a savanna near Manaus, Brazil, typically have a thick, corky, fire-resistant bark. Photo © G. T. Prance.

ABOVE: Some species of *Eucalyptus* promote fire because of their very thin, flaking bark.

BARK ECOLOGY

ABOVE: Spines on the trunk of *Eriodendron anfractuosum.*

TOP RIGHT: Palm trunks, such as this *Bactris* palm from Costa Rica, are often protected by ferocious spines.

BOTTOM RIGHT: The spinous trunk of the aptly named *Oncospermum horridum,* a palm from Sumatra.

OPPOSITE PAGE: The scaly bark of the lemon-scented gum tree, *Eucalyptus citriodora.* from Queensland, Australia, is not very fire resistant.

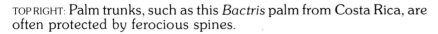

ABOVE: The neem tree, *Azadirachta indica*, from West Africa, is an important source of medicine and insecticide. Its trunk is covered with large spines.

ABOVE: The vicious spines of a red *Pereskia* cactus from Brazil.

ABOVE: The protective spines of a red silk-cotton tree, *Bombax malabaricum*, from Indochina.

TOP RIGHT: The long thin spines of a rare Australian plant, *Gyrostemon ramulosus.*

BOTTOM RIGHT: The spiny trunk of the *Astrocaryum mexicanum* palm from Panama.

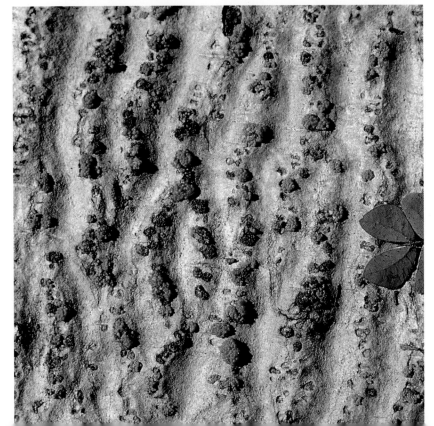

Rubber trees in a plantation at Limbe, Cameroon. Photo © G. T. Prance.

• • • • • • • • • • • •

Latexes in Bark

One of the objects which most took my attention at Pará was the Maceranduba tree, or Cow-tree, so called from its bark secreting abundance of drinkable milk.

RICHARD SPRUCE
An observation, 1849

Have you noticed the white milky sap in the stem and leaf of a dandelion? It is latex. The same substance occurs abundantly in the inner bark of many trees, especially tropical trees. It is best known for its use in rubber production, but chewing gum and various electrical insulating compounds also employ latexes.

Latex is important to the tree as a means of defense against predatory insects. Its presence in bark, the outer layer of the trunk, means that the inner wood is well protected. There are two main ways in which latex deters predatory insects: a mechanical method and a chemical method. In the mechanical method, the thick and sticky latex simply renders an insect's mouthparts ineffective by gumming them up. The chemical method poisons or repels an insect with a variety of noxious or repellant compounds.

Because of predatory pressure, plants have evolved a great variety of latexes. They have also invested a lot of energy in the production of chemical defense compounds and in the development of other means of protection. Since these defense substances occur in a wide variety of unrelated species, there are chemical and geographic variations in latex. This diversity has meant that people around the world have found numerous uses for these naturally occurring substances.

Any milky sap exuded by plants is called *latex*, a name derived from the Latin word for milk (*lac, lactis*). Although the name is used for a wide variety of chemical substances, latex is basically a watery liquid matrix with various substances in solution and with minute particles in suspension that give a milky appearance. It is a complex mixture of terpenoids, carbohydrates, proteins, tannins, gums, mineral oils, and waxes, which varies greatly from one species to another.

As its name suggests, latex is most frequently milky. There are, however, clear-colored latexes, and Guttiferae, a large, tropical plant family, has a characteristic yellow or orange latex.

Latex is produced in special cells or rows of cells called *lacticifers*, and can be found in many parts of a plant. It can easily be observed in a dandelion (*Taraxacum*) or a milkweed (*Asclepias*). However, tropical trees, such as the rubber tree, are the biggest producers of latex.

Rubber is actually produced by more than 2000 species of plants belonging to several families. Commercial rubber is produced largely from the Brazilian or Pará rubber tree, *Hevea brasiliensis*, of the spurge family, Euphorbiaceae. A source of rubber that used to be important in the United States is the desert bush guayule (*Parthenium argentata*). In recent years, it has regained importance, but 90 percent of the world's rubber is from *Hevea* trees.

Chemically, rubber latex is a polyterpene consisting of 50 to 6000 isoprene units. It is known as an isomer, a chemical compound that differs from another only in the arrangement of the atoms in the molecule, but not in its chemical structure. Rubber is in the cis arrangement, which means its atoms are on the same side. Balata, the other isomer, has the trans, or opposite-side, arrangement and, as a consequence, does not have the same elasticity as rubber.

In rubber trees, latex is produced in a network of vessels in the phloem or inner bark. This makes it easily obtainable by tapping the tree. Since the chains of cells come together at an angle of 30 degrees to vertical, the cuts are made in spirals or at an angle to cross the lactifers. Tapping, however, is a skillful procedure because the bark must be cut to exactly the right depth to sever the lactifers without going through the inner bark and causing permanent damage to the tree. Latex flow is gradual, but increases with continued tapping, so it is easy to tap productively. However, flow is seasonal, and thus trees are tapped for about 6 months of each year.

Once latex has been gathered, it must be fixed to avoid decomposition. This is done either by coagulation or by keeping the latex in liquid form with ammonium hydroxide as a fixative. In the interior of Amazonia, latex is usually coagulated by passing it over acid wood smoke. If not coagulated quickly, rubber latex turns rancid. It can also be coagulated chemically by acetic or formic acid. In its coagulated form, it can he shipped to the factories for processing.

Rubber is one of the plant products which has a long and interesting association with people. The pre-Columbian populations of the Caribbean and northern South America used rubber, made from *Castilla*, a member of the fig family, to make balls, shoes, containers, and coat fabrics. Christopher Columbus returned from Haiti with some rubber balls made from *Castilla*, but they were simply regarded as a curiosity. It was not until years later that Westerners began to find uses for rubber. The famous British scientist Joseph Priestly (1733–1804) is credited with naming it. He discovered it would rub out or erase the writing of a pencil, and so he called it rubber. Erasers are still called *rubbers* in Britain.

In 1823 a New Englander introduced local fishermen to "gum shoes" made from Amazon rubber, but the shoes were not a great success since in winter they cracked in the cold and snow and had to be warmed by the stove, and in summer they became sticky. That same year, the Scotsman Charles MacIntosh began to coat cloth with rubber and so invented the raincoat. He dissolved rubber in naptha, then coated the cloth with it. The naptha evaporated leaving rubber-impregnated waterproof material. Raincoats are still known as macintoshes in Britain, although they no longer contain rubber.

The French traveler and scientist Charles de la Condamine, as a result of his travels to Brazil, was the first person to draw attention to rubber's potential. In 1736 he made a presentation about rubber to the French Academy of Sciences.

The U.S. inventor Charles Goodyear from New Haven, Connecticut, made the greatest discovery about rubber. In 1839, after experimenting for several years with ways to prevent rubber from becoming sticky and melted in hot weather and brittle in cold weather, he discovered the process of vulcanization, which stabilizes rubber by heating it with sulphur.

With this discovery, numerous uses for rubber were found, including the manufacture of tires. After the Scottish engineer John Dunlop patented the pneumatic tire for bicycles in 1888, rubber was in great demand, and the need for rubber continued to grow with the inventions of the automobile and airplane.

The worldwide demand for rubber which began in the mid-nineteenth century triggered a rubber boom which was to alter drastically the course of life in Amazonia. Rubber barons sent out gatherers into the remotest regions to tap the wild trees of *Hevea brasiliensis*. They also enslaved entire Indian tribes in their merciless quest for "white gold." One rubber baron, Julio C. Arana of Peru, owner of the notorious firm Casa Arana, is credited with causing the death of 40,000 Indians, or 80 percent of the total population, on the Peruvian-Colombian border between 1890 and 1910.

As the market for rubber increased, the rubber barons developed a lavish life style and turned the Amazon cities of Manaus and Belém into prosperous centers of culture. Opera houses were built in European style, and mansions decorated with marble and tiles from Europe were common. Even the Customs House in Manaus was erected with bricks from England. Manaus boasted the first electric trolly service in the Americas, and its wealthy citizens sent their clothes to Paris to be laundered. All this was a result of the profits in a bark product from wild trees.

In 1872 Joseph Hooker, director of the Royal Botanic Gardens, Kew, England, sent Henry Alexander Wickham to Brazil to obtain rubber seeds, which Hooker planned to grow somewhere in the British Empire. Four years later Wickham shipped 70,000 seeds via a steamer to Kew. Contrary to popular belief, the seeds were not smuggled out; Wickham had obtained clearance for his cargo.

Because rubber seeds remain viable for only a short time, only 9000 survived the long transatlantic journey and germinated at Kew. The seedlings were shipped in portable greenhouses (Wardian cases) to Sri Lanka and from there to Singapore. A few survived and became the basis of the Asiatic rubber plantations in Malaysia, Java, and Sumatra.

In the Amazon, rubber does not flourish in plantations because the trees are attacked by a leaf rust fungus (*Microcyclus ulei*). The disease spreads easily from tree to tree in plantations, but does not spread so readily among wild trees that are distributed throughout a species-diverse forest. Fortunately for Hooker, the seeds he sent to Asia did not carry the disease, and so rubber plantations flourished there. The first Asiatic commercial production of rubber began in 1910 with a yield of 11,000 tons.

Three years later Asiatic production equalled that of Amazonia, and the Brazilian monopoly was broken. Prices fell and the Amazon boom towns became ghost towns. Not until World War II did the Amazon rubber industry recover a bit when Asiatic supplies were cut off. Rubber from wild trees is still an important product of Amazonia, but it is just one of many sources of regional revenue.

Among the other species of trees that produce a usable rubber is the genus *Castilla* in the fig family, Moraceae. Native to tropical America, this tree yields an elastic product similar to the rubber of the Brazilian rubber trees. In South America, its rubber is frequently called *caoutchouc*.

There is still a large demand for natural rubber, although there are now many synthetic rubbers. Radial tires, for example, require at least 40 percent rubber, and aircraft and tractor tires must be almost pure rubber. Natural rubber will obviously increase in importance in the future as world petroleum supplies diminish and push the price of synthetics higher than the price of natural rubber.

Gutta-percha latex, a rubberlike gum, comes from the milky latex of the bark of many trees of Sapotaceae, the sapodilla family. It differs chemically from rubber in that the isoprene units are linked in the trans configuration rather than in the cis arrangement. The result is that gutta-percha latexes are not elastic like rubber, but are hard and brittle.

True gutta-percha comes from the balata tree, *Palaquium gutta*, a member of the sapodilla family, native to the South Pacific. The trees were felled in the past to extract latex; currently, however, they are tapped, and so the species is no longer being eliminated, but rather is being wisely exploited and maintained. South American balata is extracted from species of the genus *Manilkara*. The products of balata trees are mainly used as insulators and to coat underground and marine cables. They are also used in golf balls, various surgical appliances, and in some adhesives.

The best-known and most used gutta-percha latex is chicle, which is the base for chewing gum. The original chewing gum came from Mexico and Guatemala. Today, chewing gum is a mixture of natural latex products and synthetics.

Chicle is extracted from the same species of tree that produces the popular tropical fruit sapodilla (*Achras zapota*). *Chicleros*, or latex gatherers, make zig-zag gashes from the top of the tree trunk to the bottom. A good tree yields 60 pounds (27 kilograms) of latex, but then must be left for a period of several years before it is tapped again. Tapping too frequently led to the death of many chicle trees. The latex is collected from wild trees during the rainy season when the sap is flowing in greater quantities.

Another latex-bearing tree that has been tapped for its gutta-percha, which is used in masticants, is the sôrva tree (*Couma* sp.) of the Amazon forest, a member of Apocynaceae. Unfortunately, even today sôrva trees are felled to extract the latex. Each year, as gatherers penetrate further into the forest, the species of *Couma* are becoming rare and threatened with extinction.

Tree bark contains latex as an important contribution to the tree's own health and safety. However, with careful use this same latex can benefit humankind without causing damage to the trees that produce it.

ABOVE: The lichen-covered trunk of a rubber tree, *Hevea brasiliensis.*
The outer bark hides the lactifers.

RIGHT: Rubber latex is collected by slitting the bark to the correct depth
and allowing the liquid to run into a bowl. Photo © G. T. Prance.

LATEXES IN BARK

ABOVE: Balls of crude rubber formed by the smoke coagulation process, ready for export from the area of production on the Purus River in Amazonian Brazil. Photo © G. T. Prance.

RIGHT: A ball of crude rubber in the processs of coagulation. Latex is poured on the ball as it spins over smoke and then sets. Photo © G. T. Prance.

60

OPPOSITE PAGE, TOP: The bark of the Indian rubber tree, *Ficus elastica*, contains latex for rubber.

OPPOSITE PAGE. BOTTOM LEFT: A crisscross pattern from tapping a balata tree near Puerto Morelos, Yucatan Peninsula, Mexico. The tree behind is the useful legume *Gliricidia sepium*, which is grown widely as shade for cocoa trees, as a living fence, and for firewood. Photo © Colin Hughes.

OPPOSITE PAGE. BOTTOM RIGHT: A Wardian case of rubber tree seedlings. This type of portable greenhouse was used by The Royal Botanic Gardens, Kew, to transport rubber seedlings from England to tropical Asia to begin the plantations. Photo © G. T. Prance.

ABOVE: The rough bark of the manna gum tree, *Eucalyptus viminalis*, secretes a sweet, gummy substance that is eaten by the local population. This specimen is growing at 7000 (2100 meters) feet above sea level near Canberra, Australia.

• • • • • • • • • • • • •

Resins in Bark

*And they sat down to eat bread: and they lifted
their eyes and looked, and, behold a company of
Ishmaelites came from Gilead with their camels
bearing spicery and balm and myrrh, going to carry
it down to Egypt.*

GENESIS 37:35

Is there no balm in Gilead, no physician there?

JEREMIAH 9:22

*Then [the Magi] opened their treasures and offered
[the infant Jesus] gifts: gold, frankincense and
myrrh.*

MATTHEW 2:11

You may have touched the
trunk of a pine tree and found a sticky, thick substance oozing from
its wounds, or seen a viscous material seeping out of a freshly cut
pine log. Resin, like latex, occurs mainly in the inner bark of trees.
Through the years, people have found many uses for this natural
substance. It is an ingredient of varnishes, shellac, and lacquers,
and is the source of such incense as copal, frankincense, and
myrrh.

Resin is important to the tree as a defensive substance in the bark. It protects the inner wood against predatory insects in the same ways that latex deters them: by a mechanical method that gums up the insect's mouth, and by a chemical method that poisons or repels a predator.

In addition to this protective role, resin also helps the tree by healing wounds. Often when a branch breaks off a resin-producing tree, the scar is rapidly covered by resin which seals it and protects the tree from fungal infection.

Resin occurs in all genera of coniferous plants, but is very abundant only in the pines and the araucarias. Pines contain more resin than other conifers, and together the two groups comprise the majority of resin-bearing trees species in the temperate regions. In the tropics, however, over 10 percent of the tree species contain resin, including many tropical legumes (Leguminosae), burseras (Burseraceae), and dipterocarps (Dipterocarpaceae). Resin is important for the survival of these rainforest trees, which require protection against the many diverse insect predators.

Resin occurs in canals through the bark, although these canals also occur within the wood of many resiniferous species and in their leaves and flowers. It is produced in the epithelial or border cells which line these canals. Resin is a complicated chemical mixture of terpenoids, some of which are volatile. Monoterpenes and sesquiterpenes are volatile components which often give the characteristic smell to a resin, while diterpenes and triterpenes are nonvolatile components of resin. Because resins vary greatly in chemical composition, it is often possible to identify one species from another by its resin chemistry.

Resin is usually a sticky, perfumed liquid when it is first secreted. On contact with air, it hardens into a brittle glasslike substance that typically is tasteless and odorless. It is generally light yellow to dark brown in color, flammable, and burns with a smoky flame. Resin is also soluble in ether, alcohol, and other organic solvents.

Unless it comes in contact with an organic solvent, resin is unlikely to be destroyed; consequently, it is easily preserved or fossilized. Fossil resin is called amber. True amber comes from resin of extinct species of pine that once grew in what is now the Baltic region. It has been found in large quantities along the Baltic coast of Germany, and in lesser quantities in Sicily, the Black Sea, and other parts of Europe. Some amber deposits date back 300 million years. This fossilized resin enables researchers to compare the chemistry of ancient resin with that of modern pines.

Amber often has bubbles of air, insects, leaves, or slivers of wood embedded in it. The best-preserved fossils of many insects, some of which are extinct species, are among those found in amber. The study of organisms embedded in ancient resin is one of resin's most interesting aspects, but unfortunately, much of this history has been lost because the beauty of amber has meant that it has been used for jewelry and ornaments.

Over 5000 years ago, amber was used as a barter item by the early Bronze Age people. For some, amber had religious significance; others believed it had curative properties, or wore it as a protection against evil. Similar properties have been attributed to amber by many primitive peoples.

The Greeks, Phoenicians, and Romans valued amber and set up trade routes across Europe to obtain it. In fact, one of the reasons the Romans colonized the northern extremes of their empire was to maintain access to amber. They used it for beads, amulets, pendants, and carved ornaments, many of which have been found in Roman archaeological sites. The Romans also observed that when amber is rubbed with a cloth, it becomes charged with static electricity, just like bakelite, an artificial resin. This characteristic added to the mystery and folklore which surrounded amber.

The value of amber held long after Roman times. In the earlier days of Europe, amber was the property of the finder, but in fourteenth-century Germany, the Rittenorder of Knights declared themselves the owners of all amber. Anyone found holding it was punished by hanging. The order established guilds of amber turners, built warehouses, and monopolized trading. Today, amber continues to be mined along the Baltic coast, and it is still a valued product. It is used for many things besides jewelry, such as cigar and cigarette holders, pipe mouthpieces, and statues and ornaments. It has also been used for varnishes.

Other parts of the world have deposits of fossilized resin and in each place, because of its clear, gemlike appearance and highly polishable surface, it is also used for jewelry. Amber is found in Burma, Mexico, and on various Caribbean islands. The amber from the New World tropics is usually from the resin of various members of the bean or legume family.

The best-known fossil resin from Mexico and south is copal, which comes from the leguminous tree *Hymenaea courbaril* or stinky toe. It has been used as an incense, as a source of ornamentation, and by the varnish and lacquer industry. It was an important item to the Mayans who burned it as an incense offering to their gods. This copal usually came from the resin of the members of the bursera family. African copal comes mainly from another legume in the genus *Copaifera*, and Manila copal comes from the Asiatic conifer *Agathis*.

The well-known biblical incenses, frankincense and myrrh, are both from the resin of trees of the bursera family, which is one of the most important sources of resin. Frankincense comes from the bark of trees in the genus *Boswellia*, especially *B. carteri*, a native of northeast Africa. To obtain any quantity of resin, it is necessary to wound the trees. A thin layer of bark is peeled off and the resin flows. Frankincense is still used today as an incense by many Orthodox and Catholic churches.

Commiphora opobalsamum, a species related to the one that produces myrrh, is a native of Africa and Asia. Its resin is the mecca, or balm of Gilead, which is also much used medicinally and in perfumes. The Ishmaelites, ancestors to the Arabs, were transporting balm of Gilead to Egypt when they met the sons of Israel and bought Joseph into slavery. The ancient Hebrews also were familiar with the medicinal uses of balm of Gilead.

Myrrh comes from the resin of *Commiphora* trees, a genus native to the area from Somaliland to India. The resin is produced naturally in large teardrops without artificially wounding the tree, but greater quantities flow when the bark is pierced. In addition to its use as an incense, myrrh has been used by dentists as a medicine to reduce pain from dental cavities.

Probably the most important and largest industry based on resin has been that of varnish and lacquer. Both fossil and contemporary resins are used for varnish. This use of resin is also ancient. The Egyptians coated the cases of mummies with varnish made from soft resin dissolved in oil, and varnishing has long been an important type of decoration in the Orient.

Varnish is made by dissolving resin in a solvent, such as linseed or tung oil, which is then diluted with turpentine. The mixture can be spread in thin coats to form a hard, glossy protective film which is used on furniture, ornaments, oars, musical instruments, and many other objects. The Stradivarius violin was coated with a slow-drying linseed oil varnish. Today many useful synthetic varnishes exist, but there are still high-quality varnishes which use only natural resins.

Benzoin is a type of resin from various species of *Styrax* in Thailand, Malaysia, and Indonesia. It is an exudate of the pierced bark, which forms "tears" of the reddish to yellowish resin. Benzoin is extremely fragrant and so is used extensively in perfumes and incense. It contains a high quantity of benzoic acid, which gives it medicinal properties as an antiseptic and as an inhalant for the treatment of respiratory diseases, two uses that are common for many other resins. Siam benzoin is regarded as the best because it has the highest content of benzoic acid.

Mastic is the resin of a member of the sumac family, *Pistacia lentiscus*, which grows around the Mediterranean Sea. When the bark of this tree is injured, it exudes transparent drops of resin that are pale yellow to green in color. Mastic is used in medicine as an astringent and for the varnish industry. Mastic liquor is flavored with this resin mixed with anise.

By definition, a resin thickens and hardens on contact with air. However, some trees produce liquid resins, called oleoresins. The best known of these is turpentine, which comes from various species of fir and other conifers. Oleoresins are generally produced in the sapwood rather than in the bark of a tree, and so they are mentioned only briefly here. Turpentine consists of essential oils, largely pinene, from which camphor is made, plus a type of resin called rosin. The oil is separated from the rosin, which remains, by steam distillation. This residue of the turpentine industry is hard, brittle, and tasteless, and has a slight odor of pine. Rosin, also known as calophony, is probably best known to anyone who has learned to play the violin, since it is used to treat the bows. It is also used in varnish, paint, sealing wax, adhesives, cement, soaps, sizing for paper, and medicines. Gymnasts and other athletes rub powdered rosin on their hands and the soles of their shoes to prevent slipping.

There are countless other local uses for the many types of resin produced by the bark of trees around the world. Amazonian Indians burn the resin of a species of *Protium*, which comes from the incense tree of the bursera family, for light. They have learned that the resin of another species of *Protium* makes a good waterproof caulking material for their boats. Resins are among the most useful of all bark products, and people around the world have been ingenious in exploiting this common natural resource.

OPPOSITE PAGE: The bark of *Bursera simaruba*, the gumbo-limbo tree, from Belize, contains a resinous sap which protects the tree from insects.

ABOVE: Resin oozes from wounds in a *Pachyrhynchus orbifer* tree caused by a snout beetle. Resin flows from tree wounds to heal the tree and prevent infection by disease.

BELOW RIGHT: This piece of amber from the Baltic Sea area contains the fossil of a fly.

OPPOSITE PAGE: Resin in the bark of *Agathis dammara*, the Amboina pine, from Ambon, Indonesia, is the source of Manila copal.

ABOVE: *Pinus massoniana.* a source of resin in Cenxi County, China. Photo © G. T. Prance.

ABOVE: Tapping resin from *Pinus massoniana* in Cenxi County, China. Photo © G. T. Prance.

RESINS IN BARK

TOP: Pine resin in Chinese factory, Cenxi County, China. Photo © G. T. Prance.

BOTTOM: Resin exuded from wound in pine branch, Grand Canyon National Park, Arizona. Photo © G. T. Prance.

ABOVE: Beads of resin form around a wound in *Samanea saman*, the saman or monkeypod tree, of the West Indies.

Many types of medicinal barks are sold in the market of Iquitos, Peru. Smell is obviously an important factor for this customer. Photo © G. T. Prance.

• • • • • • • • • • • • •

CHAPTER 7

Bark Medicines and Poisons

For the arrows of the Almighty are within me;
Their poison my spirit drinks.

JOB 6:4

Next him, the huntsman, Amycus he kill'd
In darts invenom'd and in poison skill'd

VIRGIL

He [Odysseus] came seeking the deadly drug,
wherewith to anoint his bronze-tipped arrows. He
did not give it to Odysseus—but my father gave him
the drug, for he loved him exceedingly.

HOMER, *Odyssey I*

It is not surprising that bark is an important source of medicinal and poisonous compounds as many of the most interesting chemical compounds in a tree are in the bark. These substances are present in the bark while they are being transported from one part of the tree to another, or as a defense against predators, especially against bark-boring insects. Some of the most toxic substances are those which are medicinally potent, too, so it is hard to distinguish between poisons and medicines derived from bark. For example, as we shall see below, the arrow poison employed by South American Indians is derived from the same source as the modern drug curare.

Most indigenous cultures around the world have discovered that bark is a useful source of medicinal compounds. Many of the brews used by native peoples for the treatment of a wide range of diseases come from the bark of trees. Several times as we have travelled around the tropical forests of South America, the teas made from the bark of trees by kindly native people have proved more effective in curing minor fevers or dysentery than the pills in our medicine box. It is significant, however, that it is not only folk medicine which derives curative ingredients from bark. Several well-known cures used in modern medicine owe their existence to the bark of trees. The history of the treatment of malaria, for example, would have been very different if quinine had not been discovered in the bark of the cinchona tree of South America. In this chapter we shall consider a few examples of medicinal barks rather than give a lengthy catalog of indigenous uses.

Witch hazel is a lotion that is familiar to many North American families. It contains an oil extracted from the twig bark and leaves of the witch hazel tree, *Hamamelis virginiana,* familiar to many gardeners. Long before European settlers arrived in the New World, Native Americans were using witch hazel for the treatment of many ailments and for muscle toning. The Menomini of Wisconsin brewed a witch hazel extract which athletes rubbed on their legs prior to playing lacrosse. The Chippewas of Michigan used the inner bark of the witch hazel tree as an emetic for the treatment of poisoning and as a topical remedy for the treatment of any skin trouble. They also used witch hazel as a wash for irritated eyes. The Potawatomi Indians placed witch hazel bark in water with hot rocks to create a steam bath for the treatment of sore muscles.

There are hundreds of records of the use of witch hazel for burns, bruises, blisters, hemorrhoids, frostbite, internal bleeding, sore eyes, and other medicinal purposes. Whether or not it is an effective medicine, witch hazel remains an important product even today. Most people have experienced the soothing feeling and pleasant smell of witch hazel applied on a bruise resulting from some athletic event. This bark product is also used in aftershave lotions for its soothing and cooling effect on the skin and in mouthwashes, eye drops, and various skin lotions.

Witch hazel oil is usually extracted by steam distillation of young twigs of the plant, which are boiled in vats of water. The oil is carried off in the steam, which is then cooled, collected, and bottled.

Many superstitions have been attached to this plant because of its name "witch hazel." The name was coined by early European settlers in the United States who recognized the similarity between the leaves of this plant and those of two trees from their homeland, namely the English witch elm and the hazel nut. Many of the supersti-

tions connected with both the witch elm and the hazel nut were transferred with the name to the American witch hazel. In spite of its name, the European witch elm has nothing to do with witches. The name was derived from *wyches,* or chests, which were made from the wood of the witch elm in Medieval England.

Witch hazel is an unusual plant because it flowers in November when other plants are leafless and dormant for the winter. This unusual flowering time has contributed to the mystery and resulting superstitions connected with this tree. The flowering time also makes it and its Asiatic relative attractive garden shrubs, since they flower and add a pleasing scent to the air at a time when little else is in bloom. Witch hazel bark continues to be a useful commercial product as it has been for many centuries.

For many years, the most popular and widely used laxative was extracted from the western buckthorn or cascara sagrada tree (*Rhamnus purshiana*) in northwestern United States and adjacent Canada. It is still an ingredient of some laxatives, although its importance has diminished in the array of laxatives currently available, many of which have a much preferred, less drastic effect than pure cascara.

Native Americans considered this bark sacred, and so the early Spanish missionary priests gave it the common name, cascara sagrada, which means sacred bark. Like the witch hazel, this member of the buckthorn family was used by Native Americans as a medicinal plant long before it was first described by Lewis and Clark in 1805. It was not until 1890 that it was first cut commercially around Salem, Oregon, where the tree is common still.

The inner bark of the cascara sagrada tree is bright yellow when it is first peeled, but on exposure to air it soon oxidizes to a dark color. Like many native medicines, it is extremely bitter tasting and nauseating when chewed. There is no doubt about the efficacy of cascara as an emetic, due to the presence of a chemical called hydroxymethylanthraquinone.

Cascara bark is harvested from May to August while the sap is running and the bark strips off easily. Trees more than 3 inches (7 centimeters) in diameter are cut, but a stump is carefully left about 12 inches (30 centimeters) above the ground. The stumps coppice and produce sprouts from which new trees develop. The bark is peeled from the fallen tree and taken to a ventilated warehouse for drying, where it will yield up to 150 pounds (68 kilograms). It is crushed, broken, and sacked for shipping to processors who usually store it for one year before the extract is prepared and bottled. This maturing time improves the extract's qualities as a tonic and laxative.

Another equally bitter-tasting bark that has proven to be an effective medicine is quinine. It comes from the genus *Cinchona,* in the coffee family, Rubiaceae. The bark of this Andean genus of trees contains thirty alkaloids, quinine, being one of them. Quinine is of great importance because for many years it was the only known cure for malaria. It is still the most effective cure for various drug-resistant strains of malaria.

The history of quinine is long and complicated, and full of political intrigue and deceit. As with many other plants of economic value, people have not been willing to divulge the secrets of quinine and its uses, or even share its seeds. Consequently, legends have embellished the facts.

Malaria has long been a worldwide health problem. It has been responsible for many deaths, including those of Alexander the Great and Oliver Cromwell. By the seventeenth century, the need for a cure was so urgent that it brought with it potential political and economic power. This spurred individuals and organizations to exploit any advantages, and led to attempts to establish a monopoly on quinine.

The bark of the quinine tree was probably used as a medicine by native populations in the Andes long before the Spanish Conquest. It is uncertain whether malaria existed there prior to the conquest, and the exact uses of quinine by the original Andean inhabitants are not known. The plant became important worldwide when someone discovered that drinking the powdered bark with water cured the malaria, or "Ague" as it was called, that ravaged the early Spanish armies and settlers.

The genus was named *Cinchona* by the founder of modern plant and animal nomenclature, Carolus Linnaeus. He named it after the wife of the Viceroy of Peru, the Countess of Chinchon, who, according to one of the apocryphal stories attached to quinine bark, was cured of malaria in 1638 through drinking the bark of the quinine tree after all else had failed to cure her.

A few years later the Jesuits discovered the use of quinine for malaria. Their organization began to buy up all supplies of the bark from Colombia and Peru, which they then sold in Europe through subtle advertising. They had a virtual monopoly of the product for the first years of its commerical use, from 1651–1660. Quinine became known as "Jesuits' bark" and consequently was scorned and denigrated by reformers and physicians alike in such places as the protestant England of King Charles II. The king, however, was cured of a malaria attack through the deceit of an entrepreneural apothecary, Robert Talbor, who claimed to have a secret cure for malaria and joined the attack on Jesuits' bark. When he successfully cured the sovereign, Talbor was knighted and elected to the Royal College of Physicians. He later cured the Dauphin of King Louis XIV of France and the Queen of Spain. It was only later, after Talbor had made a fortune and changed his name to Talbot, that he disclosed his secret remedy was quinine bark mixed with wine!

The continued exploitation of quinine from the wild trees of Bolivia, Peru, and Colombia gradually made the product more difficult to find and threatened the very existence of the species. This led, in the nineteenth century, to efforts to cultivate *Cinchona* in other parts of the world and so break the Spanish monopoly. After various attempts to introduce *Cinchona* elsewhere, the Dutch tried in Java and the British tried in India and Ceylon. Both governments were aware of the amount of money wasted on importing trees that either died or produced stock low in quinine content.

The Andean quinine monopoly came to an end through the actions of an English trader living on the shores of Lake Titicaca in Bolivia. Charles Ledger, for whom one of the species of *Cinchona* was later named, found that the bark which yielded the highest quinine content came from Bolivia. He eventually obtained seeds of the high-yielding trees in 1865 and sent them to his brother in England. The British Indian Colonial office spurned his offer to sell them, so he sold some of the seeds instead to the Dutch East India Company. The seeds were planted in Java and by 1873 quinine plantations were established. By 1884 Java took over the quinine bark market from South America and the Dutch colonial government had a virtual monopoly of the supply until the fall of Java to the Japanese in World War II.

With the main supply source in Japanese hands, the Allies had to obtain quinine elsewhere to treat their troops fighting in tropical areas. Fortunately, the severity of the Dutch monopoly and price controls had tempted others to try to reintroduce quinine into the New World long before the war, so some of the material introduced to Guatemala in 1934 was ready for use when it was most needed. Much research was done to improve the cultivation of quinine in the New World, and many young U.S. botanists spent their war service in the jungles of Ecuador and Peru providing seeds for the new intensive breeding program of quinine.

The material originally exported from Bolivia with a high yield of quinine (10–13 percent) turned out to be a new species that was subsequently named *Cinchona ledgeriana*. It is a rather slow-growing species that is easily attacked by disease, especially in the seedling stage. The Dutch overcame this problem by grafting onto stronger stock. *Cinchona* bark is harvested by uprooting the trees at about 12 years of age, when they have reached a diameter of about 4 inches (10 centimeters), and stripping it from both the stems and the roots. In some cases only the trunk is used and the stump is allowed to sprout to regenerate.

Malaria is still the number-one killer in tropical areas. Although many synthetic drugs are now used to treat it, quinine is important in resistant cases. Wtih its long and often shady history, quinine bark remains a commercial product today because of its other uses in medicines, mouthwashes, and beverages such as tonic water.

The search for medicines in bark continues today as many pharmaceutical companies analyze and test bark chemicals. The bark of the Pacific yew (*Taxus brevifolia*), for example, has been found to be effective for the treatment of ovarian and other forms of cancer.

Some of the chemical compounds found in bark are toxic. As the quotations at the beginning of this chapter indicate, the use of these compounds in poison arrows is an ancient custom often referred to in classical literature. People around the world have discovered that an arrow or blowgun dart is a more effective weapon when it is coated with a deadly poison.

The best-known poison, curare, is also the source of the drug curarine, a medicine. Like witch hazel and cascara, the story of curarine begins with native peoples. For many hundreds of years, perhaps even thousands, the Amazon Indians have poisoned their blowgun darts and arrows with a variety of toxic substances, mainly from the barks of trees and vines. The most effective arrow poisons are the curares, variable and complicated mixtures of bark extracts from a number of plant species. Curares are distinguished from other arrow poisons by their chemical composition. They are a mixture of strychnine, a highly poisonous alkaloid found in the bark of several plants in the vine genus *Strychnos,* and curarine, an alkaloid found in species of the genera *Abuta, Chondodendron,* and *Curarea,* of the Menispermaceae, the moonseed family.

Each Indian tribe varies the recipe for curare by using different species of *Strychnos* and Menispermaceae, together with a variety of other barks as admixtures. However, the presence of curarizing alkaloids in curare shows clearly in this poison's muscle-relaxing effect, an effect which distinguishes curare from other arrow poisons.

The differences in curares were recognized early in scientific research. In 1896 the scientist R. Boehm classified curare into three types based on the kind of container in which the Indian tribes stored it: tubo-curare was stored in long bamboo tubes, calabash-curare in gourdlike calabash shells, and pot curare in ceramic pots. The tribal storage customs coincide approximately with three chemical compositions: tubo-curares are made mainly from Menispermaceae and thus contain bisbenzylisoquinoline alkaloids, calabash curares consist mainly of *Strychnos* bark and so have bisindole alkaloids, and pot curares are a mixture of roughly equal quantities of *Strychnos* and Menispermaceae.

The literature on curare shows that in addition to the known alkaloid-bearing plants, each tribe adds various other plants. Some of these extra barks contribute in a specific way, such as making the paste stickier. Others may not contribute to the effect of the arrow poison.

The Jarawara Indians of the Purus River regions of Central Amazonian Brazil prepare pot curare. This Arawak tribe uses poisonous blowgun darts to hunt small game. The poison is prepared from a mixture of the bark of four species of plants: ira (*Strychnos solimoesana*) and bicava (*Curarea toxicofera*) in the Menispermaceae are the two principal ingredients. They are used in larger proportions than the other two ingredients, and more *Strychnos* is used than *Curarea.* To this basic mixture, the Jarawara add two other plants: boa (*Duguetia latifolia*) in the annona family, and balala (*Guarea*) in the mahogany family. The four barks are mixed with water and heated in a ceramic pot. The mixture is boiled down to a

sticky residue, which is then used to coat blowgun darts. The wet darts are passed through a fire to dry the poison and then are ready for use. The remaining poison is stored in a small gourd for future use.

When Sir Walter Raleigh returned from his Orinoco expedition in 1595, he was the first European to bring back news about curare and its paralyzing effect. It took over 300 years for the medicinal application of curare to be discovered. As scientists began to analyze curare's chemistry and experiment with it, they discovered it was a muscle relaxant when used in small doses. Consequently, by the late nineteenth century curare was used in France to treat epilepsy. It was not until 1930 that medical attention was turned to the potential uses of curare through the research of Dr. Ranyard West of Oxford University in England, who successfully treated tetanus cases in dogs with injections of curare. By March 1946, at a meeting of the Section of Anesthesia of the Royal Society of Medicine, two scientists, Drs. Gray and Halton, presented the results of their experiment with d-tubocurarine chloride in anesthesia which they called a "milestone in anesthesis." Dr. Halton found that curare used with pentothal relaxed the patient and prevented spasms. It also contributed to a quick and trouble-free convalescence after surgery. Thus curare, first useful as a toxic substance, entered the modern pharmacopeia as an important drug. Curarine is also used for treatment of chronic spastic conditions and as a powerful sedative.

The yoco vine of the western Amazon is the only known bark source of caffeine. Most of our caffeine for daily stimulus comes from fruits, such as coffee and cocoa beans, or from leaves, such as tea or mate. Yoco (*Paullinia yoco*) belongs to the soapwort family, Sapindaceae, and is related to the guaraná plant (*Paullinia cupana*). Guaraná fruits are an important source of caffeine as a popular Brazilian soft drink and as a stimulant for various tribes of Indians. The yoco plant differs because the caffeine is used by four tribes in a small area of Amazonian Colombia in the Putumayo regions: the Coreghajes, Ingas, Kofans, and Siouas.

The yoco plant is a woody vine or bushrope whose stems grow to about 3 inches (7.6 centimeters) in diameter. To collect the plant, the Indians fell a group of trees that are entangled by a yoco vine. They then cut the stems into pieces 1–3 feet (0.3–0.9 meters) long, which they bundle and transport back to their houses. The vine is stored in cool areas of the house for daily use as required.

To obtain the caffeine, the Indians rasp off the entire bark, including the phloem. The raspings are squeezed to express the caffeine-rich sap into cold water. (If the vines are dried out, they are soaked before this process.) The sap of about 3.6–4 ounces (90–100 grams) of scraped bark is added to a calabash bowl of water for one dose.

The custom of the Indians is to take a dose of yoco at the start of their day at 5–6 A.M., and then to eat no food until lunch time. This caffeine-rich beverage acts as a stimulant, and also deadens hunger pangs and helps to avoid fatigue. Yoco is a regular part of the life of a Kofan Indian just as a morning cup of coffee is a regular part of the life of many Europeans and North Americans. The Indians also use yoco as a medicine. It is a febrifuge for malaria fevers, and is used in the treatment of various stomach disorders. The yoco serves as an example of one of the numerous barks that are used by native peoples around the world as part of their pharmacopeia.

Bark is an important source of fish poison for native peoples. Sometimes the leaves of trees or herbs or the fruits of such trees as pequiá (*Caryocar glabrum*) are used as a fish poison, but often bark is the source of the poison. The bark most commonly used in Amazonia comes from another liana species of the legume genus, *Lonchocarpus*.

Many fish poisons, including *Lonchocarpus*, affect the membranes of the fish gills so that they no longer function. Technically the fish is asphyxiated rather than poisoned. The poison is placed in small streams or pools that are in some cases dammed for the occasion. The fish that are affected by the poison float to the surface and are collected in baskets or leaves. As the poison dilutes in a flowing stream, fish will actually recover if they are not collected initially. When a group of Indians is fishing by this method, they collect and eat fish of all sizes and the very small fish are considered a special delicacy.

The *Lonchocarpus* vine is used by several tribes of Amazon Indians. They find the vine in the forest, cut it into lengths of about 12 inches (30 centimeters), and transport it to the fishing spot. Many tribes, such as the Maku and the Jarawara, cultivate this vine in their fields. The vine is beaten with a hard stick to separate the bark and make the sap run. It is then thrown into the stream where the Indians want to catch fish.

Fish poisoning is usually a community effort by the tribe. In the Maku tribe, some of the men prepare the poison and place it in the stream, while upstream other men stir up the mud to make the stream muddier. Downstream a whole group of women and children gather the fish excitedly, while others may be making palm leaf baskets in which to place the catch. When the fishing is over, there is a big party at which the catch is roasted over the fires and a great celebration takes place.

With the Maku Indians, such fishing parties are occasional events, not a daily source of food supply. The Indians are careful not to poison the same stream too frequently. They often walk a long way through the forest and over many suitable streams before the right spot is found. They will not use a stream that has been recently used. If this stewardship and awareness of the limited natural resources of the environment had been transmitted to later settlers of the Amazon, extinction would not threaten the Amazon manatee, the giant turtle (*Podocnemis expansa*), the jaguar, and many other Amazon animals.

Lonchocarpus acts as a fish poison because it is rich in rotenone, a chemical familiar in Western civilizations as an ingredient of insecticides. The *Lonchocarpus* vine is cultivated in Amazonian Peru to supply the pest control industry, but with the advent of petrochemical insecticides, *Lonchocarpus'* rotenone is used less now than it was in the 1940s. It may become important again as petroleum supplies diminish and the price of petrochemicals rises.

These few examples illustrate some of the ways people have put to good use many of the highly toxic chemical compounds which nature put in bark for the protection of forest trees. Lives have been lost from bark-poisoned arrows, but many more have been saved by bark-derived medicines.

ABOVE: The bark and leaves of the upas tree, *Antiaris toxicaria*, in the breadfruit family, are highly toxic and can be fatal if handled improperly. In Java the poisonous sap is used to coat arrows.

BELOW: Each pile of bark for sale in this stall at the Iquitos market, Peru, equals one dose of this medicine. Photo © G. T. Prance.

BARK MEDICINES AND POISONS

Jagua Indian in Peru with a blowgun, the darts of which are poisoned with the bark product curare. Photo © G. T. Prance.

• • • • • • • • • • • •

CHAPTER 8

Hallucinogenic Bark

Several tribes of Amazonian Indians use bark as a source of hallucinogenic substances for various rituals. These narcotic compounds, which are in the bark to defend the tree against predatory insects, are powerful hallucinogens in people. In this chapter we shall examine two of these bark-derived narcotics.

The ucuuba tree (*Virola theiodora*), a member of the nutmeg family, is the most widely used source of hallucinogenic bark. The Yanomami of northern Brazil and southern Venezuela have developed its use to a greater extent than any other tribe, although many other tribes also use *Virola* bark. The Yanomami select a *Virola* tree in the forest and slit its bark horizontally as high up as possible. They then strip the bark off longitudinally in large sections and place the strips on a wooden frame over a fire which is built near the tree. The heat causes the dark red resin to ooze out copiously. The resin is brushed off with a finger into a receptacle such as a ceramic pot, or more usually today, a saucepan. The process is repeated a second time, to obtain more resin, before discarding the bark. When there is sufficient resin in the container, it is immediately boiled dry over the fire. The resulting crust in the bottom of the pan is pulverized with a hard stick into a fine powder.

This powder can be taken as a hallucinogen in its pure form, or it can be mixed with other plants which add aroma to the snuff.

Virola resin is also used by the Yanomami as an arrow poison. Arrow tips are dipped into the pot of concentrated resin while it is still liquid and sticky. These arrowheads serve two purposes: they are used in hunting to kill game and as a place to store snuff. This dual use among Yanomami Indians at Tototobi was first reported by ethnobotanists Richard E. Schultes and Bo Holmstedt in 1968.

In some Yanomami villages, snuff is stored in bamboo-shoot containers rather than on arrowheads. It is used at many different ceremonies, such as when welcoming a group of visitors from another tribe. The Sanema group of Yanomami use *Virola* snuff in two ways: witch doctors take it to induce a trance before treating a patient, and the men of the tribe take it in a ceremony for the dead. The Sanemas do not appear to use snuff except during these and other ceremonial occasions.

At the village of Auaris, a member of the Sanema tribe died from what appeared to be a common cold—an ailment against which the Indians have little or no resistance. The ceremony following a death is long and complicated. At least one ceremony is held for each person who dies, including infants, and in some cases, more than one ceremony is held. The description which follows concentrates on the use of the *Virola* bark snuff and does not attempt to cover the entire ceremony in full detail.

The ceremony begins with most of the men from the tribe going on a hunt for big game: tapir, pigs, spider monkey, and capybaras. This hunt lasts about 12 days. While it is taking place, one man goes out to invite a group from another village. The visiting group arrives before the hunters have returned and spends most of its time drinking a highly fermented liquid made from cassava flour (*Manihot*). When the hunters return, they join in the drinking. The intensity of the ceremonies that follow depends on the success of the hunt.

The Indians dance every night for 5 to 10 days. On one night the men (and often the boys) dance, and on another the women dance, dressed in palm leaf skirts.

One evening during the ceremonies, the snuff is taken. Two or three older men gather in the middle of the community dwelling, called a maloca, and begin to scrape the power from the arrowheads that have been coated with *Virola* resin in the forest. First, one man sniffs the powder, then all the men take a pinch and sniff it, or have someone blow it into their nostrils with a small blowpipe.

After all the men have used the snuff, the whole group gathers in the center of the maloca and begins to dance, holding their weapons (bows, arrows, or axes) over their heads. They shout and, according to an informant, they also commune with the spirits while under the influence of the narcotic.

The dancing is followed by an incredible chest-beating ceremony. If anyone has a grievance or is upset, he takes it out physically on somebody else in the group. Usually the men pair up or form small groups. One man offers his chest as a target to the other man, who hits it as hard as he can with his fist, a rock, or a piece of pointed metal. After one hit, the men change places so the other man gets a turn to hit his partner. The men continue taking turns until one of the pair has had enough and capitulates. The blows are hard, and blood often runs, but the man who is struck does not seem to flinch; he is apparently anesthetized by the narcotic.

Following the chest-hitting ritual, each member squats down, puts his arms around another's neck, and all shout in one another's ears. It is quite deafening just to be in the maloca. When a peak of sweat and excitement has been reached, the bone ashes of the deceased are poured on the fire in the maloca. The shouting gradually dies down as the effect of the drug diminishes.

The Paumari Indians, who live over 1000 miles (1613 kilometers) distant from the Yanomami in the upper reaches of the Purus River, south of the main Amazon, use *Virola* snuff and have their own set of associated rituals. The Bora Indians of Peru also use it, but they prepare it differently. There they chip off the hard, brittle outer bark from each strip with a machete, leaving the inner bark and phloem which they call *tcu-bee-ho-o*. The oxidized resin gives the bark a red-brown color. The inner bark mass is pounded on a log with a wooden mallet or hard stick until it is shredded. The shreds are cut into small pieces and soaked in cold water. After approximately 2 hours, the water turns dark brown. It is brought to a boil, and kept at boiling point for about an hour. Next, the bits of shredded bark are removed, and the liquid is boiled down to a rich chocolate-colored paste. The paste can be used as it is, or stored in pellets that are rolled in the ash filtrate salt of the leaves of a palm tree.

Various chemists have analyzed the constituents of *Virola* bark and the snuff which it yields. Both substances have been found to contain tryptamines, powerful hallucinogens that are related to LSD. The snuff contains high concentrations of the chemical 5-methoxy-N, N-dimethyltryptamine. The effects of taking *Virola* snuff include excitability, twitching of the facial muscles, nausea, and hallucinations followed by a deep and disturbed sleep. This is a potent bark.

Ayahuasca is probably the best-known hallucinogen derived from bark. It comes from the bark of various vines in the malpighia family (Malphighiaceae), principally from the appropriately named *Banisteriopsis inebrians* and its close relative *B. caapi*. These plants are large woody lianas or vines that are abundant in the forest of western Amazonia. They are much used by the Indians of that region, especially by shamans in ritualistic healing rites. The use of Malphighiaceous beverages, called ayahuasca in Spanish-speaking countries, has now been documented in a number of tribes in Peru, Ecuador, Colombia, and Brazil.

Like the *Virola* bark hallucinogen, *Banisteriopsis* is used either pure, or with a mixture of other leaves. The difference between the two hallucinogens is that ayahuasca is a beverage whereas *Virola* is a snuff. Ayahuasca is prepared by boiling the stems or bark of one or more species of *Banisteriopsis* in water, together with leaves of either *B. rusbyana* or a small shrub in the coffee family, *Psychotria viridis*. The mixture is boiled for about 6 hours until a rust-brown, bitter-tasting, tealike liquid is produced. It is then allowed to cool before it is drunk or bottled and corked.

Chemical analysis of *Banisteriopsis* has shown that the vines contain the hallucinatory compound harmaline and harmine, and the leaves contain the same substance as the *Virola* bark, N, N-dimethyltryptamine (DMT). *Psychotria psychotriaefolia,* the admixture for the *Banisteriopsis* drink in Ecuador, has been found to contain N, N-dimethyltryptamine. It is, therefore, to be expected that *Psychotria viridis* may likewise contain this tryptamine.

The use of the genus *Banisteriopsis* as the principal hallucinogenic beverage originated with the Indian tribes of western Amazonia. However, its use has spread into urban cultures in both Peru and Brazil. Local healers in the towns of the Peruvian Amazon use it, as do practicants of various spiritualist cults in the state of Acre in Amazonian Brazil. Its spread was made famous by the book, *Wizard of the Upper Amazon,* by F. Bruce Lamb. This is an amazing account of a young Peruvian boy, Manuel Cordova-Rios, who was captured by the Amahuaca Indians and eventually trained as a shaman. His training sessions under the influence of ayahuasca are recounted vividly. When Cordova-Rios eventually escaped and returned to Western culture, he became a renowned regional healer or *curandero.* Around Iquitos, Peru, there are still many such curanderos who use ayahuasca to give them their magical healing powers.

This bark-derived drug is drunk as a hallucinatory beverage in the Brazilian town of Tarauacá in the state of Acre. Nowadays, the drink is used primarily by the local Brazilian population, although the beverage is obviously of Indian origin and is still drunk by the Indians who inhabit the upper region of the Rio Tarauacá. When questioned, many inhabitants of Tarauacá admit to having experimented with the beverage at least once, and some families, including children, drink it regularly, apparently without harm. The population refers to the beverage as *cipó* (the Portuguese word for *liana);* no one uses the more widely known name *uasca* (or *ayahuasca* in Peru). Perhaps they use the ambiguous word for liana because of the secretiveness shown by many who use the drink. One family reported that they merely take cipó in connection with spirit worship, a cult that is extremely common and growing in the region.

The use of the beverage has spread from Tarauacá through Acre to the state capital, Rio Branco, where it is referred to as *uasca.* Several clandestine groups connected with the spirit-worshipping sects meet to drink the narcotic in much the same way these groups meet in Tarauacá. It is interesting that the Brazilian users of hallucinogens have adapted the indigenous tribal use of a narcotic for their own purposes, attaching their own folklore to its use and developing their own ceremony rather than using the Indian ones. Cipó and its ceremonies have become a part of the Acre culture.

The natives of Tarauacá insist that both plants, *Psychotria* and *Banisteriopsis,* are needed for the beverage to have the desired effect. Some claim that using the drink without the *Psychotria* leaves results in a vastly inferior hallucinatory experience.

Psychotria is a common species in the forests near Tarauacá. *Banisteriopsis* is much harder to find because use has severely depleted natural sources. A few people in Tarauacá cultivate *Banisteriopsis* to have it more readily available. The vine is easy to propagate, and when a small section of the root is planted, it sprouts and grows rapidly.

Apart from the use in spirit-worship, individuals in Tarauacá and other towns in the region frequently gather to drink cipó. The group begins by taking a large quantity of the drink, except for one man who serves as the *mestre* (or master of ceremonies) and is in charge; he does not drink on that occasion. While background music is played, everyone in the group shuts their eyes and waits for the hallucinogen to take effect. During this time, some vomit up the drink.

The hallucinations then begin. The job of the *mestre* is to bring anyone out of the hallucinatory experience should it be a bad one. He does this either by touching the person, which usually works, or by putting a strong-smelling substance, such as ammonia, or in some cases, a leaf of an unidentified plant, under the person's nostrils. Intoxicated individuals brought out of a trance need only close their eyes again to resume the hallucinations. The group continues under the supervision of the *mestre* until the effect of the hallucinogen wears off. During the entire process, loud music is usually playing in the room.

Those who have taken the beverage described particularly bright colors and large-sized objects and animals, mostly snakes and jaguars. Some people reported seeing cities that they had never visited and described ocean liners and large stores in considerable detail.

An Air Force captain once showed a cowboy film and a documentary on Brazil to the Indians at Tarauacá. He said the Indians were distinctly disappointed by the movies as they had seen all that and more while under the influence of cipó. In the future they intended to use cipó instead.

The bark of some trees can be powerful snuff!

RIGHT: A Yanomami Indian peels the bark of a *Virola* tree to obtain resin for snuff. Photo © G. T. Prance.

BELOW: *Virola* bark is then heated over a fire, causing the resin to ooze out. Photo © G. T. Prance.

The bark of many lianas (woody, tropical vines) contains hallucinatory chemical compounds. This hanging liana from the Amazonian rain forest near Manaus, Brazil, has killed its host.

BELOW: The Yanomami Indians boil *Virola* resin to remove all the liquid, then pulverize it. The resulting powder, a hallucinogenic snuff, is used pure or mixed with leaves of a *Justicia* plant. Photo © G. T. Prance.

HALLUCINOGENIC BARK

HALLUCINOGENIC BARK

• • • • • • • • • • • •

CHAPTER 9

Flavors From Bark

The Lord spake unto Moses: "Take thou also unto thee principal spices, of pure myrrh five hundred shekels, and of sweet cinnamon half so much . . . and of cassia five hundred shekels . . . And thou shalt make of it an oil of holy ointment . . . And thou shalt anoint the tabernacle of the congregation therewith and the ark of testimony."

EXODUS 30:23–26

Tree bark does not appear to be very appetizing. However, as we have already seen, the inner bark of a tree is a laboratory full of many interesting chemicals, some of which have been used as flavors for food and beverages. This best-known bark flavor is cinnamon, but there are numerous others used locally by indigenous people around the world. These flavor barks have generally been used medicinally first. An appreciation of their taste has subsequently resulted in using the bark in foods and drinks for its flavor.

Many people have enjoyed the flavor of cinnamon in cakes, cookies, or fruit pies, with applesauce and in mulled wine, hot chocolate, or some other beverages. True cinnamon comes from the inner bark of *Cinnamomum zeylanicum,* a tree native to Sri Lanka and southern India. It is one of the most ancient spices, and is mentioned in the Bible. In those days it was harvested from wild trees which grew to a height of 60 feet (18 meters). Cultivation of cinnamon trees did not begin until about 1770.

Another species in the genus, *Cinnamomum cassia,* is native to Indo-China. Much of the cinnamon that is marketed comes from the cassia tree. It is an even older spice since records show that it was used in China in 2500 B.C. It has a stronger and harsher flavor than true cinnamon, which has a delicate and refined taste.

Although cinnamon originated in Sri Lanka, today it is cultivated widely in other parts of the world, especially in Java, Indonesia, East Africa, and the West Indies. It is grown in plantations where the plants are maintained as shrubs only 7 feet (2 meters) tall. The young trees are allowed to grow for 3 years before the main stem is cut back. This stimulates the growth of many stump sprouts which are left to grow for 2 or 3 years. The bark from these coppice shoots is harvested in the rainy season, when it is easily removed because the cambium is active at that time. Ten medium-sized cinnamon tree stumps yield approximately 1 pound (½ kilogram) of dried bark from each harvest. The stumps resprout and can be harvested again every 2 or 3 years. This method of management enables a tree to be productive for over 100 years.

The cinnamon gatherers of Sri Lanka collect bundles of the sticks or stump sprouts during the morning, and spend the rest of the day with the de-barking process. The bark is slit open longitudinally on opposite sides of the stem with a special curved, sharp knife. It is stripped off and the bark strips are laid aside to ferment for 1 or 2 days to enable separation of the outer and inner bark. The outer corky bark is then easily scraped off with a broad, blunt knife and discarded. The remaining inner bark or phloem is sorted into three quality classes according to thickness of bark and brightness of color. It is cut into uniform lengths or quills of 3.5 feet (1 meter) from which the familiar cinnamon sticks are formed.

The flavor of cinnamon is largely due to a phenolic compound called cinnamic adelhyde. The bark contains about 1 percent of the volatile oil that gives it the flavor, and this oil contains 55–75 percent cinnamic aldehyde. It is the subtle mixture of other compounds that gives true cinnamon its delicate and superior taste over cassia cinnamon.

Bitters have also been used to flavor drinks. On a hot summer evening many people have enjoyed angostura in their beverage. This flavor comes from the bark of the South American tree *Galipea cusparia,* which is native to the Orinoco region of Venezuela. Like many flavor sources, this one is used as a medicine by the local people. They make a tea of the bark, which is an effective febrifuge because of the glycosides in the bark.

The bitter-tasting substance can be obtained in one of two ways: either in an alcohol extract to yield a tincture containing the bitter glycosides and other aromatic substances, or through stem distillation of the bark which yields oil of angostura bark. The principal aromatic substance is a sesquiterpene alcohol called galipol.

True angostura bark is used where it grows, but it is not an ingredient of the main product marketed as "angostura bitters." The marketed substance contains gentian root, bitter orange peel, cinnamon bark, and a mixture of other aromatic herbs. Other bitters contain quinine, a medicinal bark.

Sassafras bark, from the North American tree species *Sassafras albidum,* has a history of use that goes back to the discovery of the New World. It has been an important item of commerce and a much-used medicine and flavoring. It no longer is as important as it once was, partly because recent medical research has shown that safrole, the principal flavor component of sassafras, is carcinogenic.

Long before safrole's carcinogenic nature was discovered, Europeans knew sassafras better than any other North American species on account of its purported medicinal properties. It was first brought to Europe by the Spaniards who called it *salsafras,* their name for saxifrage, on account of its similar medicinal properities. Later the English name *sassafras* appeared as a transliteration of the Spanish name. By 1549, the famous Spanish physician Monardes had produced the first account of the medicinal properties of sassafras roots and bark. Many earlier explorers, including Sir Francis Drake, took loads of sassafras bark and wood back to Europe. It was, however, Germany that developed the greatest demand for sassafras as a medicine.

Sassafras was also known in Europe for its scented wood used in fine furniture. The wood became popular because it was well-known that no insects would attack it, a characteristic which clearly demonstrates the role of aromatic compounds, such as safrole, in bark and wood, as natural defenders of the tree against insect predators.

Most seventeenth-century herbals extol the medicinal properties of sassafras. For example, the 1633 edition of the herbal of John Gerard, edited by Thomas Johnson, called sassafras the "ague tree." Gerard stated that "the root boiled in water to the color of claret wine and drank for certain days, helpeth the dropsie, removeth stopping of the liver and cureth agues and long fevres. It comforts feeble stomach and causes good appetite."

In North America, sassafras bark became popular as a tea, and the root bark became popular as the principal flavor of root beer. Dried sassafras root bark was even listed in *The United States Pharmacopoeia* from 1890 to 1926 as an offical drug. But, in 1960 the National Research Council, the National Institutes of Health, and the Food and Drug Administration (FDA) reported that safrole was a cancer-causing substance. Later that year a federal regulation banned the use of sassafras in food and drug products in the United States. In 1961, scientist Fred Homburger of the Bio-Research Institute of Cambridge, Massachusetts, published a paper reporting that safrole fed to rats in doses as small as 0.1 percent caused liver tumors. The result was that from 1960 on root beer lost its distinctive taste and has never been the same.

Many other food and drug uses of sassafras officially ceased at that time. Sassafras oil is still used in soaps and cosmetics, but is no longer used in food products. Since modern medical research has found no medicinal value for sassafras oil, it is better to be prudent and avoid its use completely. Sassafras bark is still sold in health food stores, but without any label indicating that it is tea. By not indicating the use of the bark, marketers have found a loophole in the FDA regulations. Although various health food and plant medicine writers continue to extol sassafras today, it is now strongly recommended to avoid the use of this once-popular bark flavor and follow the advice of modern research that has demonstrated clearly its carcinogenic nature.

This discovery has meant that it is no longer safe to drink a tea that is popular with some Amazonian Indian tribes and with many other Amazon residents. This tea is made from the bark of *Ocotea pretiosa,* another species of the same plant family as sassafras, the laurel family (Lauraceae). Its taste, which is reminiscent of sassafras tea, comes from an active ingredient in its flavorful bark, namely safrole, the carcinogen of sassafras bark.

There are countless other local tree barks used as flavors around the world. One example is the bark used in mavi, the well-known drink of Puerto Rico, the Virgin Islands, Hispaniola, and other islands in the Caribbean. Mavi is made from the bark of various species of Rhamnaceae, especially of *Colubrina elliptica.* The bark is boiled in water and cooled before it is allowed to ferment for a short time. Essential for the preparation of mavi is the starter, which contains the micro-organisms that cause the type of fermentation necessary to create the drink, just as homemade yogurt must be started or yeast added to most alcoholic beverages. The recipes for mavi are quite varied from island to island. In some areas, various leaves are added to give it a strong herbal taste, but in Puerto Rico it is made from pure *Colubrina* bark. It has a distinctive taste which is reminiscent of ginger beer, and is a most refreshing drink in the hot Caribbean climate.

The barks of some species of trees have brought gustatory pleasure to many people in many different places around the world. Some of them are harmless and enjoyable, such as cinnamon; others are noxious, like sassafras.

OPPOSITE PAGE: The plaquelike bark of the camphor tree, *Cinnamomum camphora,* a relative of the cinnamon tree, contains camphor, a spice used in flavorings, as a perfume in soaps, and as an irritant and stimulant in medicine.

FLAVORS FROM BARK

ABOVE: The aromatic bark of the bay berry, *Pimenta acris*, from Venezuela, yields a spice that is related to allspice.

ABOVE: This cinnamon tree, *Cinnamomum verum*, is growing in a botanical garden in Sri Lanka.

Mavi, an important fermented drink in the Caribbean, is made from the bark of the *Colubrina* tree, a member of the buckthorn family. Shown here is *Colubrina elliptica*, from Guánica, Puerto Rico. *Colubrina arborescens*, the wild coffee tree, is used elsewhere. Photo © G. T. Prance.

• • • • • • • • • • • •

CHAPTER 10

Bark Tannins

Tanning hides with bark is an ancient technique dating back at least 5000 years. The oldest evidence—a tanning yard with tools, pieces of skin and leather, acacia seed pods, and fragments of oak bark—was found by the Italian Egyptologist C. Schiaparelli and shows the Egyptians used a vegetable-tanning process similar to the one used today. Tanning is depicted in Egyptian tomb paintings from 3000 B.C., and was known to the Chinese in 1000 B.C. The Romans tanned with oak bark. Native Americans employed a variety of local plants and barks to make leather from buffalo hides. Even Neolithic people of Europe are thought to have tanned hides by immersing them in tanning bark which was placed in water holes in the ground.

Today, in an age of plastic, people still enjoy leather. It is very utilitarian because of its strength, flexibility, resistance to decay and wear, and imperviousness to water. Many people prefer to walk around on leather-soled shoes; leather purses, handbags, wallets, and belts bring much pleasure to their owners, and even the smell of a leather goods shop is savored by many. There is a great variety of leather types, due in part to different methods of tanning and to the different tree barks which can be used. Some barks will also add color or odor to the leather, so the selection of the tanning substance is crucial to the end product.

The tanning process is possible because of a property of certain chemicals, called tannins, which combine with the protein of animal skin, collagen, to produce leather, a product which is much more permanent and tougher than unprocessed skin. Tannins are mainly derived from the bark of the many species of trees that produce them. In fact, tannins are among the most important bark products.

Tannins are also acidic and very astringent. This property has made them important in folk medicine, but they are also useful in food processing, in fruit ripening, and in many beverages, especially cocoa, tea, and wine.

Another notable property of tannins is that they produce a blue or green color and precipitate with salts of iron. This has made them a major coloring ingredient of many inks. They are also used as mordants in the dyeing process.

Although tanning is an ancient industry, the actual chemicals that cause the tanning reaction were not discovered until 1790–1800 in France when tannins were finally isolated as distinct chemical compounds. Chemically, they are classified into two groups: the hydrolysable, and the condensed or nonhydrolysable tannins. Hydrolysable tannins (gallotannins) are glucosides. They contain a central core of glucose or other polyhydric alcohol with gallic acid residues attached out from the core. Condensed tannins (polyphenols) are compounds of high molecular weight, polyphenolic polymers apparently lacking sugars.

Tannins are widely distributed in the plant kingdom. Scientists E. C. Bate-Smith and C. R. Metcalfe surveyed their occurrence in over 500 species of plants from 175 families. This study showed that although tannins are more abundant in certain plant families and absent in others, they are well distributed throughout the seed plant families. They are particularly abundant in the inner bark of hemlock, oak, acacia, and mangrove trees.

Tannins also occur in lesser quantities in leaves, unripe fruit, flower buds, and wood. In India, tannins from the fruit of certain trees, such as the myrobalan nut (*Terminalia chebula* and *T. bellerica*), are used. The greatest concentration of tannins is found in galls, the abnormal growths on plants provoked by insects. Most ink tannins, for example, are gallotannins or tannins derived from galls rather than bark. The Aleppo oak (*Quercus infectoria*) is one of the main sources of gallotannins; when an insect lays an egg on one of its twigs, gall material, growing like a cancer, surrounds the egg. Tannins often account for 25–70 percent of the tissue in galls. Consequently, galls such as those found on oak trees have been used as a source of tannins. In this chapter, however, we will concentrate on the barks which yield tannins for the tanning industry.

Since tannins are so abundant in the plant kingdom, they are likely to be functionally important. Early researchers regarded them

as waste products, but nature is not wasteful; it employs energy economically to produce substances that are beneficial to the plant. It has now been shown that tannins are distasteful to many insect species; people find them bitter and astringent as do grazing mammals. Tannins depress digestion in the rumen of cattle where the digestibility of a source of food appears to be correlated with its tannin content. Like other useful chemical substances derived from plants, such as flavors, beverages, and medicines, tannins are part of the natural protection system of plants. Their role in bark is similar to that of latex and resin—defense substances to reduce animal predation. Since bark is the outer cover which protects the tree and since it also contains the vital nutrient transport system of a tree, it is most important for the continued life of the tree. It is hardly surprising, then, that bark is rich in tannins or other protective substances. Tannins also benefit trees in other ways. They heal wounds in tree trunks and prevent decay by acting as fungicides. There is evidence that they are involved in the production of cork.

Many barks from around the world have been used as a source of tannins. It would be impossible to describe all the ones used for tanning because people have discovered the most appropriate local sources for their tanning needs. A few of the important barks are highlighted here.

In colonial times in the United States, the native forests were an abundant source of tannins. Tanning was an important industry, and the first tannery was founded in 1630. By 1650 there were over 50 tanneries throughout New England, and by 1816 the tanning industry was a business of over $200 million. One reason New England, and especially Boston, became an early center for tanning was because of its proximity to one of the best sources of tannins, the hemlock bark.

Hemlock bark (*Tsuga canadensis*) contains from 10 to 12 percent tannin. It was used to tan sheepskins and heavy leather for the soles of shoes. Western hemlock (*Tsuga heterophylla*) is also rich in tannins and became a more important source with the depletion of the Canadian hemlock. The bark was removed in the spring, during sap flow, when it is easiest to separate from the tree. The four-person barking crew consisted of a spudder, a fitter, and two bucklers who stripped off chunks of bark about 4 feet (1.2 meters) in length and 18 inches (45 centimeters) wide. The bark was dried and the tannin extracted by open diffusion or by percolation.

In 1900, about 72 percent of all tannins used in the United States came from hemlock. It was the primary source of tannins for the tanning industry. In fact, it was this industry's use of hemlock bark as a source of tannin that lead to the rapid deforestation of vast areas of native hemlock forest. Today, little remains of the once majestic hemlock forests of the northeastern United States and Canada. One of the southernmost remnants still exists within New York City, in the gorge of the Bronx River in the New York Botanical Garden.

When hemlock became scarce, the tanning industry relocated

near other sources of bark, such as oak and chestnut. The oaks have been an important source of tannin in both Europe and the United States. In fact, the first tannery in the United States was founded in 1630 in Virginia using oak bark. In North America, the chestnut oak bark (*Quercus prinus*) was the most important species. Many tanneries existed in Appalachia because of the abundance of this species whose bark contains 8–14 percent tannin. The concentrated extract of tannin from this bark with 26–30 percent tannin was much used to tan heavy leathers. The black oak (*Quercus velutina*) is another important source of tannins and smaller quantities occur in the red oak (*Quercus rubra*) and the white oak (*Quercus alba*). As its common name would suggest, the Californian tanbark oak (*Lithocarpus densiflora*) was also a source of bark tannin. Its use was stimulated by the 1849 gold rush.

The bark of the American chestnut (*Castanea dentata*) was another rich source of tannin for the U.S. industry until the onslaught of the chestnut blight in the early part of the twentieth century. The supply of hemlock and oak bark became so scarce that bark was taken from dead blighted chestnut trees. By 1957 tannin production in the United States had declined so much that virtually all tannins used were imported from abroad. Imported tannin comes principally from three sources: the African wattle bark (*Acacia* species), the bark and wood of the South American *quebracho* (*Schinopsis lorentzii*), and the bark of a species of red mangrove (*Rhizophora* species).

Species of *Acacia* are rich in tannin and have become an important commercial source in Africa and Australia. Their use, however, is by no means recent; the oldest records of tanning are from ancient Egypt where *Acacia nilotica* was the source of tannins.

The Australian wattle (*Acacia decurrens*) is widely cultivated in Brazil, South and East Africa, and Sri Lanka because the bark of certain varieties contains up to 50 percent tannin and the trees grow relatively quickly (5–15 years). Leather treated with wattle tannin is solid, very firm, pinkish in color, and is much used for soles of footwear. In 1947 it was calculated that Brazil was cultivating 70 million *Acacia* trees in the state of Rio Grande do Sul. Without doubt, this genus has become one of the most cultivated sources of tannin.

Mangrove has become an increasingly important source of tannins. A species of red mangrove also grows in Florida where it has been used for the experimental extraction of tannin. Mangrove grows in tidal swamps throughout the tropics and subtropics where it forms what was long thought to be a rather useless type of forest. Recently, however, its timber has been found excellent for boat building and charcoal, and its bark is useful for tanning. Mangrove forests are important wildlife habitats for stabilizing marine estuaries and as breeding ground for crabs, fish, and other useful organisms. Nonetheless, in many parts of the world, mangrove forests are being cut down indiscriminately either for their trees or to drain the swamps and install alternative land-use sytems. Consequently, the use of mangrove as a source of tanning material has many advantages and disadvantages. Tannin is extracted commercially from mangroves in many countries especially in East Africa, Indonesia, and Central and South America.

Leather from the former Soviet Union is often tanned with birch bark (*Betula*). It is soft and fragrant due to the agreeable aroma of the essential oil in the birch bark. Good European glove leather, which is also soft, light colored, and durable, is often tanned with material from willow bark (*Salix*). New Zealand glove leather is tanned with *tanekaha* bark (*Phyllocladus trichomanoides*), which contains an orangish yellow dye in addition to the tannin.

Because tannins from different tree barks produce a different quality and color of leather, the type of tannin selected usually depends on the purpose for which the leather will be used. Leather for gloves must obviously be quite different from leather for shoe soles.

Whatever the source of tannin, we have seen in this chapter how an astringent, bitter-tasting substance produced in bark principally to deter insects is one of the most useful bark products to people around the world, whether indigenous tribes or industrial society.

FURTHER READING

Howes, F. N. 1953. *Vegetable Tanning Materials*. London: Butterworths.

Trimble, H. 1892–94. *Tannins, A Monograph on the History, Preparation, Properties, Methods of Estimation and Uses of Vegetable Astringents, With an Index of the Literature of the Subject*. 2 volumes. Philadelphia: J. B. Lippincott Company.

OPPOSITE PAGE: Red mangrove, *Rhizophora mangle*, a common plant of tropical shores is one of the major sources of tannins for the tanning industry.

BARK TANNINS

LEFT: The numerous arching roots of *Rhizophora mangle* intertwine below the surface to stabilize the tree in the soggy soil of a tidal swamp.

BELOW: Bark of *Rhizophora mangle* ready for use in tanning at São Luís, Brazil. Photo © G. T. Prance.

OPPOSITE PAGE: Known best for its papery texture, birch (*Betula*) bark is often used in the former Soviet Union to tan leather.

BARK TANNINS

BARK TANNINS

CHAPTER 11

Cork

Cork is probably the most familiar bark product in use today. Imagine the countless number of times that people have pulled a cork from a wine bottle, smelled it to judge the quality of the wine, and then settled back to relax and enjoy themselves. Imagine the innumerable celebrations at which the joyful sound of a champagne cork has been heard popping from the bottle of a sparkling drink.

As noted in Chapter 1, cork is a common feature of bark. Nevertheless, only a few species of trees produce a layer of soft spongy cork that is thick enough to be used commercially. In fact, most cork is taken from a single species, the cork oak (*Quercus suber*), a tree native to the Mediterranean region. As we shall see in this chapter, cork is used for much more than just bottle stoppers.

Cork has been used since antiquity. It was mentioned by Theophrastus (387–372 B.C.), a Greek scientist who was the first person to systematically describe plants in a nine-volume series entitled *The Plants*. The Roman writer Varro (127–116 B.C.), and later Pliny the Elder (23–79 A.D.), who wrote an extensive multi-volumed *Natural History,* both referred to cork. All three authors described uses of cork which are similar to those of today. Pliny and Horace recorded that Roman fishermen used cork floats to keep their nets buoyant as far back as the fourth century B.C. The Romans also used cork to insulate houses and beehives, as soles for sandals, as stoppers for bottles, jugs, and vases, and as larger buoys for the navigation of their ships. During the seige of Rome by the Gauls, a man managed to swim across the Tiber River with the help of cork floats.

As early as the twelfth century A.D. when Portugal was first established, laws were passed for the conservation of that nation's valuable natural resource, cork. Father Fernando Oliveira in his sixteenth-century book, *Livro da Fabrica das Naus,* wrote that cork was in great demand for naval construction, but the supply was scarce in both Spain and Portugal. Industrialization has resulted in many new uses for cork, ranging from gaskets for engines to cigarette tips, resulting in a continuing high demand for this bark product.

Thomas Jefferson, the great innovator, suggested in 1787 that cork could be grown commercially in the states of Arizona, California, Nevada, New Mexico, and Texas, but the countries of Portugal, Spain, and Algeria remain the largest producers of commercial cork. The cork oak grows wild in southern France, Spain, Portugal, Italy, Greece, and in northwest Africa—Algeria, Tunisia, and Morocco. Cork is also collected from the eastern oak (*Quercus occidentalis*) which occurs only along the Atlantic coasts of Spain and Portugal and adjacent France.

Cork is the outer bark of a tree that protects the inner bark or phellogen. Year by year, layer upon layer of cork is added to the tree. As seen in Chapter 4, cork's main function is to protect the tree. It is thought that the oaks have evolved this thick, protective coating of cork as an insulation from the hot desert winds, or siroccos, which are common in the eastern Mediterranean region. Today, in support of this idea, cork cutters avoid removing cork in the windy season, because in cutting the cork the phellogen is exposed and vulnerable. If it dies, it causes death to the trees.

Cork from wild trees is not as uniform and useful commercially as cork from trees in which the growth is managed. That is because natural cork is coarse, deeply furrowed, irregular, and full of sand grains. It can be so dense that it will not float. To obtain commercial cork, the natural cork must first be removed, then the new growth is much more uniform, and commercial cork is produced. The natural cork is removed from the lowest 30 inches (76 centimeters) of the tree when it is about 15 inches (38 centimeters) in circumference. Six to ten years later the first harvest of cork is made from this lower 30 inches (76 centimeters), and a further 18 inches (46 centimeters) of natural bark are removed above it, increasing the next harvest by that increment. Increasingly larger areas of natural bark are removed for the first five harvests. Thereafter, an elaborate system of alternating the harvest area is followed, so that only part of the trunk is subject to harvest at any one time.

Cutting cork is a skilled job; the correct amount of cork must be removed each harvest to leave the inner layer of the tree intact. If this inner layer is damaged, no regrowth will occur. Wild (natural) bark and subsequent new cork growth must be harvested evenly to leave the surface of the tree absolutely smooth and uninjured. If the cork is not removed evenly, the new layer of growth will be uneven and thus useless for commercial purposes.

A circular cut is made in the bark at the desired height, and another cut is made at ground level. The correct depth of these cuts is crucial to successful harvesting. Next, a vertical cut is made to connect the two horizontal cuts. The layer of cork is then detached from the tree with a specially shaped, bevelled hatchet handle. If the tree's circumference is 2 feet (0.6 meters) or less, the cork is usually removed in one piece, but in larger trees, two or three vertical cuts are made to remove the cork in several pieces.

Commercial cork 6 to 10 years old averages about 1 inch (2.5 centimeters) thick. It is harvested only during the season when the tree is in sap, because the layers separate more easily then. The harvest season is carefully planned to avoid the initial, large sap flow, yet to be finished before the hot winds begin. Even with skilled workers, about 2 percent of the trees are lost at each harvest.

If you examine a cork bottle stopper, you will see a series of darker brown lines running through it. These are the breathing pores or lenticels, which were described in Chapter 1. Since these pores function as small pipes carrying air into the inner bark, they could also make cork a leaky bottle stopper. However, cork cutters take care to cut cork so that the pores run horizontally rather than vertically and thus the pores do not permit the liquid to escape.

The cork we use is not the pure product direct from the trees. Once the slabs of cork have been stripped from the trees, they are boiled for 1.5 hours in long rectangular vessels to swell the bark. The boiling reduces the specific weight but increases the volume by 20 percent. This process is important to close the pores, increase the elasticity, and make cork more compact and supple. After boiling, the slabs of cork are scraped and trimmed to remove fiber and then cut into standard marketable sizes. At this stage, defective parts are removed, and the cork is graded and bundled in bales according to five classes:

Thick	31 mm or more (1.22 inches)
Ordinary	26–30 mm (1.02–1.18 inches)
Bastard	23–25 mm (0.91–0.98 inches)
Thin	22–23 m (0.87–0.91 inches)
Refuse	22 mm (0.87 inch)

The commodity market of cork is quite extensive. Cork may be sold at auctions, or in Spain and Portugal it is quite common for a buyer to purchase the produce of an entire mountainside while the bark is still on the trees. The bidding in a North African cork auction reverses the procedure followed in Western auctions. The auctioneer starts with a ridiculously high price and gradually lowers it until someone in the audience bids on it. The first person to make an offer is the buyer.

Cork is very useful since it combines many mechanical properties not found elsewhere in nature. Whereas most barks contain primarily fibers and only small amounts of cork, the bark of oak reverses the situation. Cork consists of millions of minute thick-walled cells, each with an airspace in the center. It is these air spaces which give cork bouyancy in water. A 1-inch (16-cubic centimeter) cube of cork contains approximately 2 million cells tightly bound together by resinous materials. In fact, 50 percent of the space in cork is air. Therefore, when it is compressed, cork is an elastic substance; much of the air remains in the cells, and upon release, the air pushes the cork back to its original shape. The combination of compressibility and resistance to moisture and liquid penetration makes cork an ideal stopper for bottles.

Cork has many other physical properties which make it a useful product. It is resilient, has high friction, low heat conductivity, and an ability to absorb vibration, and is a stable substance. Each of these features adds to the number of uses for cork. Since it does not conduct electricity or sound, it is a good insulation material. Heat and sound insulation are due to the air spaces in the cork cells, but cork's electrical resistance is due to the cork itself.

Much of the world's cork supply is not used as pure cork, but rather as composition, in which the cork is reduced to grounds, then glued together in blocks with a powerful natural or synthetic adhesive. Composition cork can be shaped in many ways and any thickness, depending on the use. It is used in gaskets, bottle caps, shoe innersoles, polishing wheels, acoustic tiles, and numerous other products. If it is to be used for containers of food products, care must be taken to use a tasteless and nontoxic adhesive.

Cork board differs from composition cork; it does not contain adhesives, but rather uses the natural resins in the cork itself. This product was discovered accidentally in 1892 by John Smith, who was heating small pieces of cork in a metal container when he noticed that they stuck together. Today, cork board is made by compressing ground cork in a mold at high temperatures. The natural resins bind the cork particles together into a strong board. This board has many uses, such as in machinery isolation, insulation, acoustical walls, tiles, and of course, the familiar cork bulletin boards that can be found in many homes and offices in North America.

Linoleum, which was invented by Frederick Walton in Britain in 1863, was originally a cork product. True linoleum consists of a backing of burlap or canvas overlaid with a mixture of cork ground into a fine powder and oxidized, polymerized linseed oil. The mixture of cork and the rubbery oil derivative gives a flexible sheet with a smooth surface that is a durable and easily managed floor surface.

Almost all commercial cork still comes from the original area in the Mediterranean. Nevertheless, there are many other trees beside the cork oak which have a thick layer of cork to protect them from fire. These trees are found especially in the savanna regions of the tropics (see Chapter 4). No other bark, however, combines all the favorable properties of oak bark cork. A variety of trees has been used as substitutes for the oaks. For example, the thick-barked elm, *Ulmus suberosa,* has been used, but its cork is brittle and unsatisfactory. In India, the bark of various pines, including *Pinus mercusii,* has been used for cork. In Africa, cork is taken from the bark of the *Musanga smithii,* and in South America, from *Anona glabra.*

In some cases, soft wood rather than cork has been used for bottle stoppers. Various species of willow and poplar have been used thus, as has the soft pith of elder or even sunflower. None of these substitutes can compete with genuine cork as a large-scale commercial product. Cork, therefore, remains a most important commodity for countries around the eastern half of the Mediterranean Sea.

OPPOSITE PAGE: The cork oak tree, *Quercus suber,* from Corsica, has a very thick bark. Photo © Jane Runicles.

Stacked cork harvest, southern Portugal. Photo by Karen Kirtley.

ABOVE: Harvested cork trees in southern Portugal. Photo by Karen Kirtley.

RIGHT: Recently harvested cork oak, *Quercus suber*, from Corsica, has a very thick bark. Photo © M. Sinnott.

Huitoto Indian scarlet dye made from seeds of the achiote (*Bixa orellana*) plant ready for bark painting. Photo © G. T. Prance.

• • • • • • • • • • •

CHAPTER 12

Bark Cloth

The tissue of bark can
Keep the images that I draw.

From an Ojibway poem

People around the world have discovered that the inner bark of many species of trees can be stripped and beaten to form a clothlike material. This material has been given many names, including bast cloth, bark cloth, and tapa.

Three areas of the world have been the centers of bark cloth culture: Polynesia, Central Africa, and central and northern South America. This distribution pattern—in tropical regions of the world—probably reflects the large number of tree species in these areas which have bast that is suitable for cloth making.

The history of bark cloth is difficult to trace because it is primarily a tropical product. As such, it is not very durable, and there are few archaeological remains of it. There is no doubt, however, that bark cloth production is an old craft. Some fragments in archaeological excavations indicate that bark cloth was used in Indonesia as far back as 1000 B.C.; other fragments unearthed in archaeological excavations in Peru date back to 2000 B.C. Neolithic bark cloth implements have been found in Norway, and birch bark boxes have been discovered at Port in Switzerland. Thus, we also know that bark cloth was used in the temperate regions of the world.

Chinese records from the sixth century B.C. show that bark cloth was used, and there are many subsequent records of the use of paper mulberry in Chinese history. Marco Polo was one of the early Western explorers to note the use of paper mulberry in China. The use of that plant probably spread from China through the Malay Peninsula into Indonesia and from there throughout the Pacific Islands.

Tapa, as it is known in Polynesia, attracted the attention of many early Pacific explorers because of its beautiful colors and intricate designs. Captain James Cook collected large quantities of tapa, and the naturalist accompanying him, Joseph Banks, made copious notes about it in his journal. In the eighteenth century, collections of tapa were often cut into small pieces and bound into books. The 200-year history of tapa designs is preserved in many European museums. Although these collections are small page-sized samples of larger designs, they serve to show the quality of early tapa work.

Much material for bark cloth comes from the many members of the mulberry or fig family, the Moraceae. In the Pacific region, the two most commonly used sources of bark come from this family: the paper mulberry (*Broussonetia papyrifera*) and various species of the breadfruit genus (*Artocarpus*). In fact, the paper mulberry, which is much cultivated for its use as cloth, was given its species name *papyrifera* (paper-bearing) on account of its principal use. Although the bark of paper mulberry is used more than any other bark in Polynesia and produces the best-quality cloth, the tree is not native to the Pacific region. It is actually a native tree of China, Taiwan, Japan, and Korea. Its ease of cultivation and the quality of the cloth have led to a wide use of paper mulberry.

A species of hibiscus is also a good source of bark cloth as are many species of fig. Fig trees are the main source of bark cloth in Africa (where the mgubu fig is used) and among the South American Indians. In Hawaii, a particularly strong and fibrous tapa is made from the mamaki shrub (*Pipturus albidus*), a member of the Urticaceae or nettle family.

Bark cloth is manufactured by peeling the bark, in a single piece, from the appropriate tree. Next, the outer bark is separated from the inner bark or bast. In most species it peels off cleanly, but in others some scraping may be necessary. Some groups beat out the freshly stripped bark, while others soak it in fresh or salt water before beating. Those who soak the bast do so to bleach the cloth and remove impurities. Furthermore, if the cloth is soaked for a prolonged period, small pieces can be beaten together, thus forming larger sheets without any sewing. Beating the natural bark fibers in a sodden state not only blends them together, but the thickness of the cloth can be controlled by the amount of beating it is given.

Tools, the exact methods, and the stages of preparation vary considerably from region to region and from species to species. The initial stage of the manufacturing process, for example, varies greatly from island to island in the Pacific. In Tahiti, the bark is soaked in fresh water, then the outer bark is scraped from the inner bark with a shell. In the Cook Islands, the bark is folded inside out to flatten it, and then the inner bark is pulled from the outer bark. In Mangareva, the bark is soaked in fresh or sea water for 3 days; then the inner bark is pulled from the outer bark, and any remaining pieces of the outer bark are pulled off.

The next stage in the process is also varied. In Tahiti, the bark strips are fermented in plantain leaves for 3 days and then put together in three layers to form a moist fibrous mass about 33 feet (10 meters) long and 1 foot (30 centimeters) wide. In Mangareva, the bark strips are given a preliminary soaking, rinsed in sea water and then in fresh water, before being arranged in bundles and wrapped in ti leaves to ferment. This process is repeated several times over a 3-day period.

The bast is beaten on a hard surface, such as a smooth stone or a rounded rock. Tapa "anvils" are an important part of the tapa-making process of many people. They are carved, shaped, or hollowed to serve as a drumlike instrument. In fact, tribal rhythms are beaten out as the work is done. The cloth is beaten with a variety of mallets, hammers, or sticks. Today, Amazon Indians often use the back of a machete. The beater may be round, square, or flat. It is usually grooved in some way, like a meat tenderizer, to spread the pressure of the impact. A smooth beater is only used for the final part of the process. It takes a great amount of skill to beat the bark evenly to the correct thickness, as beating it a little too hard in one place will make a hole in the delicate fabric.

Once the beating is completed, the tapa is left to dry. It is then ready for decoration. A wide range of natural dyes is used in different parts of the world, giving a spectrum of colors. The Amazon Indians use the seeds of the achiote plant (*Bixa*) to obtain a red dye, while in the Pacific islands, the turmeric, a relative of ginger whose root yields yellow to orange colors, is preferred. Mud, soil, charcoal, blood, and fruits have all been used to decorate tapa. Today, many indigenous peoples have access to paint and use artificial colors rather than natural dyes.

Tapa makers have used the cloth in a host of ways, from simple loin cloths to the most elaborate robes of kings and tribal chieftans. It is still the main fabric for the clothing of many indigenous peoples worldwide.

The most elaborately decorated examples of bark cloth of the Amazon are the tunics that were worn by the Yuracare. These beautiful garments, decorated with painted ornaments applied by means of wooden stamps, were made from the bast of a species of fig (*Ficus*). Within the Amazon, eastern Bolivia is the place in which bark cloth was most used and most popular. Its many tribes—the Chácobo, Mojo, and Morc—also used bark cloth tunics.

In the Aztec Empire, bark cloth was used as paper, to record business transactions and for writing books. In Tenochtitlan, the Aztec capital, about half a million sheets of bark paper were brought in each year as tithes. Poetry and other types of literature were written on this paper. Tragically, after the Western conquest of the Aztecs, the complete archives of Tenochtitlan were destroyed by order of Fray Juan de Zumarraya, the first bishop of Mexico. What a vast store of human knowledge and culture, stored on bark, was lost by that one mandate. The 1529 fire in the market place of Tlaleoka, where all the records were burned, is another sad comment on the Western conquest of the Americas.

Bark cloth is a verstile fabric. It has been used for simple loincloths and skirts, large draperies, and wallhangings, or in thick layers as a mattress. It receives paint and dye easily and has been used for elaborate paintings and designs. Some of the early bark tapestries are found in museums and prove that bark cloth production is a skill that has developed in many parts of the world. Various groups of indigenous peoples have developed their own distinctive, traditional designs which they paint onto their bark cloth. Sometimes it is freehand painting, but more frequently the designs are printed onto the cloth with shaped wooden blocks, leaves that have been dipped in dye, or stencils cut out of banana or pandanus leaves. Unfortunately, world travelers today do not often see the fine art of many traditional bark painters. Much of the available material is mass produced to meet the demand for tourist souvenirs; tapa cloth-makers in Fiji and the Bora Indians in Peru, for example, have turned this old art form into the production of shoddy mementos. They are careless in the production of the cloth, which is poorly beaten, and in the artwork. However, fine examples do still exist in most areas, and so it pays to be selective when looking for bark art.

Visitors to Mexico are familiar with brightly colored bark paintings, called *amate*, which decorate many of the souvenir shops. The word *amate* is derived from *amatl*, which means "paper" in the Nahuatl language. The trees from which this bark paper was originally made were also called *amate* and are a species of the fig genus (*Ficus cotinifolia, F. padifolia, F. tecolutensis*, etc.), which grows in the Mexican highlands.

Amate paper is made by a simple process. The fibrous inner bark of the tree is soaked and then boiled for 4–6 hours in water containing ash, which softens the fibers and makes them easy to separate. After rinsing, the soft bark strips are placed on a gridlike pattern on a board and beaten with a rectangular stone or *muinto*. Once the fibers have spread together evenly, the paper is placed in the sun to dry. In some places a glutinous substance taken from orchid bulbs is added to help the fibers stick together. The resulting bark paper can be dark tan, yellow, or almost white, depending on the original bark used.

Before the conquest of Mexico, amate paper was the parchment on which the ancient races made their written records. It is still used as paper in some highland villages, especially in the small town of San Pablito in the state of Puebla, where the Otomi tribe once made amate paper to cut out figures of *nahuales*, their devils and spirits. These figures still play an important role in the magic rituals of the people. Dark-colored bark figures tend to represent evil, while the light-colored ones represent good spirits.

In the state of Guerrero, amate paper is brightly decorated with graphic scenes of everyday village life. Much about village culture can be learned by looking at these "primitive" bark paintings. The best artists come from the towns of Xalitla, San Agustin Oapan, and Amegultepec.

The supply of amate bark has been depleted by overuse and by deforestation in Mexico, and today the craftsmen of San Pablito use the bark of three fast-growing secondary forest trees: *Urera baccifera* in the nettle family, *Chichicastle* or *Myriocarpa longipes* in the linden family, and especially *Jonote colorado* or *Trema micrantha* in the elm family. The latter is now being grown in plantations to supply San Pablito.

Bark cloth is used in many different rituals around the world. The Tikuna Indians of Brazil make elaborate bark cloth masks and clothes for puberty rites. Like many tribes of the northwestern part of Amazonia, including the Jivaro and Bora, the Tikuna use bark clothing and masks in many ceremonies. On the other side of the world in Malawi, bark cloth is also used in the initiation rites of girls.

In the Tikuna ceremony, the girls are secluded in a dark room for a month after their first menses to keep them from evil spirits and the influence of other people of their tribe. When the girls are released, they are chased by monkeylike figures dressed in bark outfits. These "monkeys" wear exaggeratedly large male sex organs, the tips of which are reddened with achiote, and chase the initiates in an attempt to mark them with the dye.

In Tahiti, tapa or *ahu*, as it is called, was central to the Tahitians' life. The paper mulberry plant was cultivated in their fields more than any other plant and it took up potential agricultural space. A major sign of wealth in that society was the size of the stack of tapa in a house. Each house had its own tapa-making shed where the women worked as hard to make the cloth as the men did to cultivate and protect the paper mulberry trees. Tapa was used for clothing, turbans, decorations for temple images, and long streamers which flew from war canoes. Tahitian bark cloth is decorated in many ways, but it is best known for the use of leaf and flower prints as part of the decoration.

Many of the early travelers to Polynesia, including Captain James Cook, who was one of the earliest visitors to Tahiti, were impressed with the use of this cloth. One of the first explorers to mention tapa was the Italian Antonio Pigaletta, who accompanied Magellan on his voyage around the world. Pigaletta recorded the use of bark cloth in the Spice Islands or Moluccas in 1521.

Another interesting record of the use of tapa involves the mutineers of *The Bounty* who settled on Pitcairn Island in 1789 with

Tahitian women. This colony, which was later discovered in the early nineteenth century, used tapa cloth for bedding and clothing.

Hawaii, until the latter part of the nineteenth century, was one of the cultures with the most uses for tapa. The men wore a *malo*, or loincloth, and a decorated *kihei*, or cloak of tapa, as well as plain arm and leg bands. They wore tapa sandals and decorated their hair with strips of orange-colored tapa. The women wore a *pa'u*, or skirtlike garment, and a *kihei*. They also wore hair ornaments similar to those worn by the men. For ceremonies, loincloths were dyed yellow with turmeric and were often perfumed. Bathing loincloths were soaked in oil. Tapa pendants decorated Hawaiian ceremonial helmets. The women used *pa'u* with elaborate stamped designs for their hula dance, and those of high rank wore tapa shirts of excessive length.

Tapa was used in Hawaiian houses as partitions between rooms, as a covering for the inside of the thatch, and on the walls for decorations. Sleeping tapas consisted of several layers of bark cloth sewn together; the upper layer was decorated. Tapa was also used for mosquito nets, floor mats, wick in stove lamps, and as a slow wick to retain fire.

Sheets of tapa were used at marriage ceremonies, and black tapa was used for palls at funerals. Tapa was much used in religious life, and white tapa was a taboo sign. Sheets of white and yellow tapa were used to decorate anthropomorphic figures signifying the presence of God. Tapa-draped obelisks were erected in sacred places. In addition, the Hawaiians used tapa as a dressing for wounds, material for cord and twine, and more recently, for binding books.

Similar uses for this versatile and important material from the inner bark of trees could be noted for almost any Pacific island. This bark product has proven to be cheap, versatile, and readily available to those peoples who have the ancient knowledge and skills to process it.

FURTHER READING

Brighton, W. T. 1911. " 'Ka Hana Tapa': The Story of the Manufacture of Kapa (Tapa), of Bark-Cloth, in Polynesia and Elsewhere, but Especially in the Hawaiian Islands." *Memoirs of the B. P. Bishop Museum* 3:1–273 (with an appended album of color plates).

Hagen, Victor W. von. 1944. *The Aztec and Maya Papermakers*. New York: J. J. Augustin.

Kaeppler, Adrienne L. 1975. *The Fabrics of Hawaii (Bark Cloth)*. Leighton-Sea, Essex: F. Lewis.

Kooijam, Simon. 1972. "Tapa in Polynesia." *Bishop Museum Bulletin* 234. Honolulu, Hawaii.

Nimuendaju, Curt. 1952 *The Tukuna*. Publications in American Archaeology and Ethnology, vol. 45. Berkeley and Los Angeles: University of California.

Worldwide use of bark cloth.

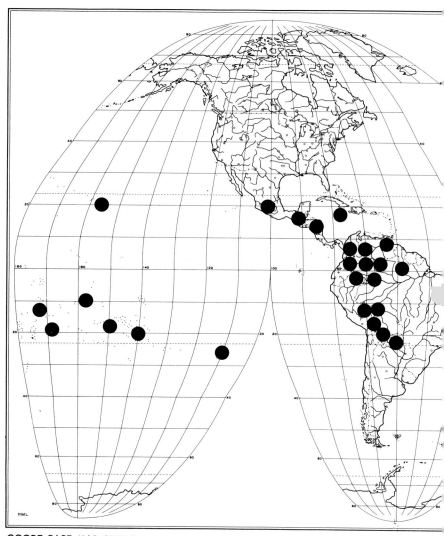

GOODE BASE MAP SERIES
DEPARTMENT OF GEOGRAPHY
THE UNIVERSITY OF CHICAGO
HENRY M. LEPPARD, EDITOR

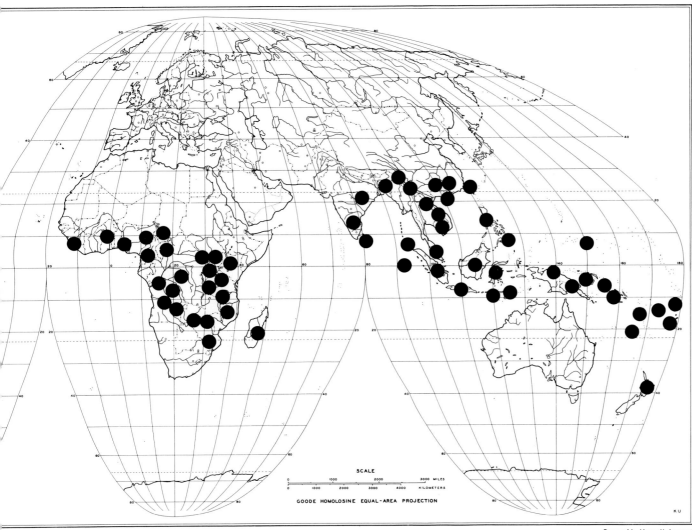

GOODE HOMOLOSINE EQUAL-AREA PROJECTION

Prepared by Henry M. Leppard
© 1961 by The University of Chicago

BARK CLOTH

ABOVE: Huitoto Indian painting a design on bark cloth. Photo © G. T. Prance.

OPPOSITE PAGE: Huitoto design on fig bark cloth. Photo © G. T. Prance.

BARK CLOTH

LEFT: Brazilian peasant removing bark in a single unit from munguba tree, *Pachira*, to use the fiber as a cloth or to caulk boats. Photo © G. T. Prance.

BELOW: Munguba fiber drying on a fence. Photo © G. T. Prance.

OPPOSITE PAGE: Bora Indians of Peru in bark clothes. Photo © G. T. Prance.

Mexican bark painting on
amate paper, a tradi-
tional Mexican art form.
Photo © G. T. Prance.

Many amate bark
paintings record scenes of
everyday village life.
Photo © G. T. Prance.

BARK CLOTH

ABOVE: Young paper mulberry trees growing in Hangzhow, China. Photo © G. T. Prance.

TOP RIGHT: The inner bark of the paper mulberry tree, *Broussonetia papyrifera*, is the source of tapa cloth in Polynesia. In the Orient, the bark is used for paper. Photo © G. T. Prance.

BOTTOM RIGHT: Although highly toxic, the strong, fibrous inner bark of the upas tree, *Antiaris toxicaria*, is used as a sacking fiber.

OPPOSITE PAGE: A Huitoto Indian woman in bark dress holding a sick baby, who has been dyed with fruit of the genip tree, *Genipa*, as part of the healing rites. Photo © G. T. Prance.

• • • • • • • • • • • •

CHAPTER 13

Bark Canoes

Their canoewes are some eight or nine pases long, and a pase and a half broad in the middest, and grow sharper and sharper toward both ends. They are very subject to overturning, if one knows not how to guide them; for they are made of barke and a Birch tree, strengthened within with little circles of wood.

Samuel Champlain, *Des sauvages, ou voyage de Samuel Champlain de Broughe fait en la France Nouvell, l'an mil six cens trois*

One of the most spectacular uses of bark is for canoes. Various peoples around the world discovered that bark could be used for making watercraft of one sort or another, but no group surpassed the skill of Native Americans who made canoes from the bark of the birch tree.

These canoes, which consist of a wooden frame covered with bark, amazed early travelers to North America. Visitors were surprised to see these lightweight vessels which could move through the water much quicker than any of their own rowing boats. In addition, bark canoes had an advantage in that navigators could see where they were going because they faced the bow.

The bark canoe was highly developed long before European

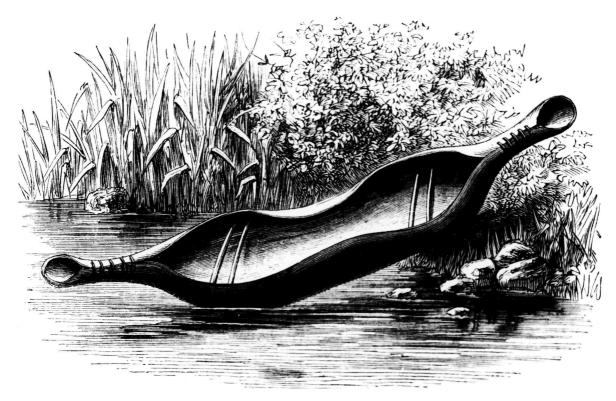

The bark canoe of the Caripuna Indians of the Madeira River region of the Amazon. From an engraving in *Up the Amazon and Madeira Rivers* by E. P. Mathews (London: Sampson Low, 1879).

explorers reached North America. Unfortunately, we do not know much of the early history or the development of prototype canoes, as they are made of light wood and bark and thus decompose rapidly, leaving no archaeological record.

The earliest known report of bark canoes is that of Caesariensis Jeusebii in *Episcopi chronicon,* who wrote of a 1509 voyage to Newfoundland, "Seven wild men were brought from the island (which is called New Land) to Rouen with the canoe . . . Their canoe is bark, which a man can lift on his shoulders with one hand." Another early report was that of the Frenchman Jacques Cartier, who in 1535 reported a bark canoe which carried 17 people. Champlain in 1603, described an Algonquin bark canoe of 8 or 9 paces (about 20–23 feet or 6–7 meters) long by 1.5 paces (4 feet or 1.3 meters) wide, near what today is Quebec City. Henry David Thoreau made two trips in bark canoes with Native American guides in 1853 and 1857. He describes them in his book *The Maine Woods.* Many other famous explorers, such as Jacques Marquette and Sir Alexander Mackenzie, used bark canoes for their travels.

Much of our present-day knowledge of bark canoes comes from Edwin Tappan Adney, an artist and writer who was born in Ohio in 1868. Adney studied native handicrafts and in 1889 built a birch

bark canoe with a Malecite named Peter Joe. During his lifetime Adney studied the canoes of many different tribes and made such detailed sketches that it is easy even today to build canoes from them. His papers and drawings are of such great historic interest that they were published in 1964 in the most detailed book in existence about bark canoes, compiled by Howard I. Chapelle, the curator of transportation at the Museum of History and Technology of the Smithsonian Institution. It is a fascinating treatment of the skilled making of the birch bark canoe.

Henri Vaillancourt of Greenville, New Hampshire, was born the same year that Adney died and learned canoe construction from Adney's book. Vaillancourt became so enamored with bark canoes that he has made a career out of their construction. He has done much to keep his craft alive today and to revive the skills which Adney so accurately cataloged in his drawings. John McPhee wrote about Vaillancourt in a book entitled *The Survival of the Bark Canoe.*

Native Americans used the bark of several different tree species for canoe shells, including spruce (*Picea*), chestnut (*Castanea dentata*), elm (*Ulmus*), basswood (*Tilia*), hickory (*Carya*), and cottonwood (*Populus*), but the bark of the paper or white birch

Betula papyrifera was unequalled. This tree, also called "the canoe birch," has a strong, waterproof and resinous bark that is ideal material for the canoe maker. The white birch tree occurs on good soil near streams, over a wide range of northern North America, from New York City north to the Hudson Bay, and west in a wide belt to the Pacific Coast. Fiber from the bark of another tree species, the basswood, (*Tilia americana*), was often used to lash the canoe frame together, and the roots of black spruce (*Picea mariana*) were used to sew the pieces of bark together.

Because the white birch tree has such a wide range in North America, prime canoe bark was available to a large number of tribes. The best canoes were made in the eastern part of the continent in what is now New Brunswick, Nova Scotia, Maine, and Quebec. Bark canoes, rather than the heavier dugouts of western Canada, were the ideal craft for use in the rivers of the eastern region. They were lightweight and could be lifted out of the water easily for the frequent portages, which are typical of water travel in the east. Some of the tribes that excelled in canoe building were the Abaanaki, Algonquin, Cree, Iroquois, Micmac, Ojibway, and the Têtes de Boule, but no group was more skillful at canoe building that the Malecite. The Beothul of Newfoundland and the Dogrib of northwestern Canada also built bark canoes. Birch bark canoes were eventually superseded through a technological advance made by the Penobscots of Maine, who were the first people to use canvas as a substitute for birch bark.

Native American canoe-makers were true craftsmen who used their own stone axes, as well as bone and wooden tools, to make canoes. Their handiwork, with primitive tools, has not been surpassed, even with the use of more-modern metal tools. They possessed the tools and the skills necessary to make the very best canoes in the world. The frame was carefully shaped and the wood bent into place with hot water. Perfect seams were firmly sealed in the bark covering with yet another bark product, the resin from the bark of the black or white spruce (*Picea mariana* or *P. glauca*), which was usually mixed with bear fat and charcoal to make a more permanent seal. Hiawatha, the sixteenth-century Native American chief about whom Henry Longfellow wrote in *The Song of Hiawatha* (1855), built a canoe using cedar branches for the frame and the "white-skin wrapper" of the birch tree as a covering. The bark he sewed together with the fibrous roots of the larch (tamarack) tree, and the seams and fissures he sealed with the resin of the fir tree.

Different tribal groups had distinct styles of canoes, all of which were drawn laboriously and cataloged by Edwin Adney. The canoe's end profile identified the tribe of the canoe builder; for example, the canoes of the Ojibway Indians had long noses. However, design also varied considerably with the function of the canoe. There were different designs for canoes on lakes, coastal waters, fast-flowing or smooth rivers, and even according to the types of portage necessary. A canoe for a solitary hunter was different from one for transporting

a family. Some canoes were broader in order to transport cargo. A canoe for use on a river with many overhanging branches had a low end profile.

Not every white birch tree has bark suitable for canoe building. Bark quality varies from tree to tree depending on such factors as soil and climate. Native Americans tested the bark of a number of trees before selecting one for a canoe. They often removed a small shingle-sized bark sample and beat it into a U-shape until it snapped. This test revealed the bark's strength and flexibility.

Bark for a canoe must be at least 1/8 inch (3 millimeters) but not more than 3/16 inch (5 millimeters) thick. This is one of the factors influencing the selection of the bark of a particular tree. If the outer layer of bark is carefully removed from the tree when the sap is flowing, the tree is not harmed. The sap protects the tree from drying up and dying so that eventually the outer bark grows back and there is another bark crop for the next generation.

Once a tree has been chosen as the source of bark, the bark is slit vertically and then peeled off in a large sheet. Summer bark, which can be recognized because it turns a much lighter color on the canoe, is not as durable as winter bark, but winter bark needs a spud of some sort to remove it. The spud is made from a piece of dry birch bark about 1 foot (30 centimeters) square. One edge is cut in a slightly rounded shape and then sharpened. It is inserted between the bark and the wood, then rocked so that the cutting edge separates the bark from the wood.

Once the bark has been peeled off a tree, it resembles a large sheet of linoleum. For transport, it is rolled along the short edge, with the bark inside on the exterior. When fresh, the bark is flexible and can be shaped easily. If the bark is not to be used immediately, it can be stored in water to keep it pliable and ready for use. If it is stored dry, as it often was, it can be made flexible again by soaking it in water for several weeks. Some groups applied heat to the bark, which melted the resins in it and produced a flexible bark.

Often canoes were built to fit the chosen piece of bark. The inside of the bark became the outside of the canoe. Canoes seldom exceeded 20 feet (6 meters) in length, although, after the arrival of fur traders in the region, extremely large canoes were made to order for them. These *canot de maitre* of the fur traders were often 36 feet (11 meters) long and weighed 600 pounds (272 kilograms). They were capable of carrying up to 4 tons (3620 kilograms) of cargo and were consequently most useful to the traders.

The canoe's frame was made from a variety of woods. White cedar (*Thuja occidentalis*) wood was preferred for the gunwales, which ran the length of the canoe, and often the ribs of a birch bark canoe were made of cedar. The cross pieces or thwarts, which hold the gunwales apart, were made from a harder wood, such as maple (*Acer saccharum* or *A. nigrum*), which was also used for paddles.

The bark was fitted onto the canoe frame by various methods. The greatest advantage of birch bark was that it could be joined together in small, odd-sized sheets to shape a hull and make a completely smooth exterior. For other barks, it was necessary to fold a crimping to make the canoe from a single piece. Birch, good stitching, and the use of resin resulted in perfectly sealed joints.

Once the canoe was completed, it was often decorated. The personal mark of the maker was included on one of the flaps at the end. Decorations were painted or scraped onto the canoe, and often porcupine quills were added to make them artistic. If the bark was removed from the tree when the sap was flowing, some sap would have stuck to the back side of the bark and turned brown when dried. Thus scraping a design on the canoe simply involved exposing the dried sap, which contrasted nicely with the lighter-colored bark. The Passamaquoddy were especially skillful at decorating their bark canoes. Today, the best birch bark decorations are done by the Cree and Montagnais of Quebec.

Bark canoes seem to have been a technical development of tribes living in the temperate regions of the Americas; the other region in which bark canoes were used extensively is the southern tip of South America in Patagonia, particularly in Tierra del Fuego. The now-extinct Alacaluf and Yahgan Indians, who lived either side of the Beagle Channel, made bark canoes as did the Chono of southern Chile, who lived in a region of fords and hilly islands where water transport was essential.

Since birch does not grow in Patagonia, the Fuegans, as the southern tribes were called, used the bark of a species of southern beech, *Nothofagus betuloides*. The epithet *betuloides* means birchlike, indicating that one of the characteristics of this beech is its rather smooth, pale-colored bark that resembles birch bark.

Fuegan canoes were constructed differently from those of the North American tribes. The Fuegans stripped the bark in spring when the sap was running. Since the southern beech bark is harder to remove than birch bark, the Fuegans used a bone chisel or a mussel-shell knife to slit the bark and then used a bone barking tool. The canoes were made of three cigar-shaped strips of beech bark, each 0.5–1 inch (1–2.5 cm) thick. These strips formed the bottom and two sides of the canoe which was 12–20 feet (3.5–6 meters) long, about 3 feet (1 meter) wide from gunwale to gunwale at the center, and about 2 feet (0.6 meters) deep.

The gunwales and five or six thwarts were made of hardwood. The frame was usually lashed together with strips of baleen (whalebone from the roof of the mouth of whales). The numerous canoe ribs were made of splits of winter bark from the beech tree. Each split was fitted and lashed in place under the gunwales. The three bark pieces of the hull were sewn together with baleen or shreddings from warmed beech saplings. The seams were caulked with stringy stems of wild celery grass or with moss mixed with mud. Unlike the northern canoes the Fuegan canoes were never completely watertight, and beech bark or seal skin bailers were an essential item in each canoe. A fireplace was set amidships and always kept alight because of the difficulty of kindling a fire in the southern climate. Braided grass ropes were used as a mooring line.

These primitive but effective bark canoes were used at the time Magellan explored the Patagonia region. In fact, it was the fires that the Yahgan Indians kept burning in their bark canoes and on the shore that caused Magellan to name the region Tierra del Fuego (the land of fire). The bark canoes persisted into the nineteenth century; however, gradually they were replaced by the dugout, which was more watertight. The Alacalufs were the first tribe to replace bark canoes with a skin-covered craft. Later, they made plank canoes from driftwood. The southern bark canoe is no longer in use, and only a few examples of it remain, such as the one in the museum of the Salesian Mission in the Chilean town of Punta Arenas. At one time, however, beech bark and its products, such as canoes, buckets, and roofing material, must have been very important, for the Yahgan name for one of the four seasons is "the time when the bark is loose."

Although there were numerous tribes living in the vast expanse between the Ojibway of North America and the Yahgan of Tierra del Fuego, few of them used bark canoes; instead, the dugut predominated. In Amazonia, many tribes know that bark could be stripped from various trees and used directly as an emergency means of water transport, but among them, only two tribes used bark canoes at the time of early exploration of the region—the Mura and the Suya of the Upper Xingu River region, in Brazil.

The Mura and Suya made 20–25 foot (6–7.5 meter) long, frameless canoes from the bark of the stinky toe tree (*Hymenaea courbaril*). This tree in the legume or bean family has a resinous bark and is also the source of South American amber. Since it is a large tree, the Indians constructed a wooden scaffolding against the trunk. Standing on it, they stripped off long rectangular pieces of bark and placed them on low wooden trestles over a fire. The heat softened the bark and caused the resin to flow. In this state the softened bark could be manipulated; the edges were bent upwards, one end was bent into a pointed prow and the other end, the stern, was bent inwards. Both ends were bound with vines, and holes and cracks were filled with beeswax or clay. These canoes, which took only one day to construct, were made next to the tree from which the bark was removed. When completed, the canoe was carried to the river on the shoulders of several men, who padded their shoulders with a protective cushion of fiber or bark. The advantage of these canoes was that they could be made quickly and used immediately. When not in use, these bark canoes were submerged to hide them from enemy tribes and to protect them from drying up and cracking.

There are other reports of South American Indian groups using similar canoes. There were certainly bark canoes among the Arecuna of the Guianas. Many tribes that originally used bark canoes replaced them at an early date with the fire-hollowed dugout.

The birch bark of North America and the beech bark of South

America were useful for much more than making canoes. They provided a flexible, waterproof material that could be used in many ways. Both the woodland tribes of the northern states and the Patagonian tribes in South America used bark as a housing material. A wooden frame tied together with vines, roots, or bark fiber was covered with birch or beech bark, respectively, according to the region, to make huts. In the north, the huts were either dome-shaped or triangular (tepees), while the Patagonian huts were shaped like domes or beehives.

The Ojibway and other woodland tribes used birch bark to wrap the bodies of the dead for burial. Some tribes made bark utensils and containers of many different designs. The elaborately decorated bark boxes of the northern tribes, which are ornamented with porcupine quills, have now become tourist items. The Fuegans carried water in bark buckets and also boiled fish in them by placing hot stones in the bucket. Green bark buckets, often made of birch, were used for cooking over low fires. The Hurons of Canada stored fish for winter provisions in large bark vats. The women made birch bark baskets. Birch bark was a writing material, and it was important in Huron medicine.

The discovery of birch bark for canoes and utensils changed the lives of the northern woodland tribes. The canoes were fast, resilient, and light to carry. When the people became more mobile, they lost the 1000-year-old tradition of pottery-making, and it was replaced by birch bark technology. The lighter birch bark containers were not as cumbersome to carry and therefore a new emphasis on movement was possible. Birch bark was certainly one of the most vital substances to the life of the northern tribes, while its southern counterpart, beech bark, enabled the Fuegans to live in the hostile climate of the Patagonian region.

FURTHER READING

Adney, Edwin T., and Howard I. Chapelle. 1964. *The Bark Canoes and Skin Boats of North America.* Washington, D.C.: Smithsonian Institution.

Gidmak, David. 1980. *The Indian Crafts of William and May Commanda.* New York: McGraw-Hill.

McPhee, John. 1975. *The Survival of the Bark Canoe.* New York: Warner Books.

OPPOSITE PAGE: Peeling off a piece of bark from a birch tree, *Betula papyrifera.* Photo © Judith Schmidt.

ABOVE: Birch trees with bark removed. The sap, which has dried black, protects the tree until a new covering grows over. Photo © Judith Schmidt.

ABOVE: A Montagnais carrying rolls of birch bark. Photo © Judith Schmidt.

BELOW AND RIGHT: The frame of a Native American canoe was typically made of cedar or maple wood. Photos © Judith Schmidt.

LEFT: Designs were either painted on the finished canoe or, as in this Abaanaki canoe, scraped into the bark. Carefully scraping the bark exposes the dried, brown sap. Photo © Judith Schmidt.

• • • • • • • • • • • • •

CHAPTER 14

Fiber, Fuel, Mulch, and Other Uses of Bark

As secure as an elephant bound with a baobab rope.

Swahili proverb

Bark is available in all forested areas of the world. Wherever this abundant resource occurs, ingenuity has found many uses for it. Bark has been used in many different ways because of its availability, and also because of its diversity. The Norwegians, for example, roof their houses with bark, the Lapps make clothes with birch bark, and the Amazon Indians construct canoes with bark. The beech tree has long been a favorite for bark graffiti writers. It was such a custom that must have caused William Shakespeare to write in *As you like it:*

> Run, run, Orlando; carve on every tree
> The fair, the chaste, and unexpressive she.

A sample of these miscellaneous uses for bark—among indigenous tribal peoples as well as in modern industrial societies—will be discussed in this chapter.

In the timber industry, bark has been thought of as a waste product that must be removed to process the desired product, wood. As a result, much of "waste" bark has been burned off or used for landfill. In 1970, about 200 million cubic feet (5.66 million cubic meters) were produced by the timber industry, but the bulk of it, 69 percent, was treated as waste; 23 percent was used as an industrial fuel and for charcoal, 4 percent as a domestic fuel, 1 percent for fiber products, and 3 percent for miscellaneous uses such as mulch.

Since 1970, the tendency has been to use more of the bark and waste less. The advent of fiberboard, particle board, and chipboard, has reduced wastage. Fiberboard is made from used pulp, to which binding adhesive compounds are added. The mixture is pressed, under heat, into sheets. Hardboard and insulation board, the products of this process, contain up to 15 percent bark. Particle board is made from wood chips mixed with glues and also contains a significant percentage of bark. Waste bark has also been used in the manufacture of shingles, sheathing paper, carpet liners, and deadening felts.

Bark is increasingly used as a soil conditioner, a mulch, and for garden pathways. As soil conditioner, it increases the porosity of the soil by trapping air and water in its matrix. Because of its porous structure, bark also drains well, like peat or sphagnum moss. This characteristic makes it an excellent soil conditioner and mulch. Bark helps to produce a soil that is easy to till, which in turn permits better air and water penetration. Five million tons (2.3 tonnes) of bark are used annually on vegetable farms, not to mention the many tons used in parks, gardens, or along the slopes of highways.

One of the most important uses of waste bark is as a mulch. A mulch is any substance placed on the soil surface to prevent evaporation of water or to suppress weed growth. Mulches are helpful in preventing soil erosion. They also protect plants by moderating the soil temperature, thus reducing freezing and overheating. Ordinary bark mulch is low in nitrogen and has no value as a fertilizer, but it can be treated with fertilizers, which it then releases slowly over a long period. Bark chips are absorbant and easy to handle. If they are used for animal bedding and have been soaked with nitrogen-rich animal urine, they are excellent as a soil conditioner because they have added fertilizer value.

Landscape gardeners and horticulturists often plant trees in certain places because of the ornamental property of their barks. A winter landscape is frequently made more attractive by such features as thickets of *Cornus alba,* whose young shoots have a rich red bark in autumn and winter, or by the coral bark maple (*Acer palmatum*), whose beautiful coral-red young stems retain their brilliance throughout the winter. Paperbark maple (*Acer griseum*) creates interest in a garden with its distinctive peeling bark, which hangs on the branches in paper thin sheets, revealing the orange-colored newer bark within. The strawberry tree (*Arbutus unedo*), native of the Mediterranean and southwest Ireland, also has an attractive shreddy bark. *Prunus maackii* has a smooth-barked trunk, striking brownish yellow in color, that peels like that of a birch. The familiar white-trunked birches are often placed in gardens for the winter effect of their distinctive bark. Another tree with a beautiful white bark is the lacebark pine (*Pinus bungeana*). A native of China, it was widely cultivated in the gardens of Buddhist temples for its bark. The bark, which is brown in the young trees, is a pure white in older trees, and makes this one of the most distinctive of all pines.

Fuel is certainly the most important industrial use of bark. In fact, bark has as great a fuel value as wood. For example, burning 1 pound (½ kilogram) of dry Douglas fir sapwood yields 8500 BTUs, and burning the same amount of heartwood yields 9000 BTUs, but 1 pound of dry bark yields 10,000 BTUs. The more resinous the bark, the greater its fuel value; thus, pine bark is a rich source of energy. In the future, as petroleum supplies decline, there is no doubt that bark will become increasingly important as a source of fuel. One current problem is that pulp mills generally use water in the debarking process. The energy needed to dry the bark so it can be burned for fuel does not compensate for the amount of fuel it provides. Pulp mills and saw mills already use bark as a fuel, as does the charcoal industry, so some waste is avoided. Turning bark into charcoal reduces its weight by 25 percent and its volume by 50 percent without reducing the fuel value. It is, therefore, a more economic way of distributing bark energy.

People everywhere have sought to improve the aesthetic quality of their lives by the use of color and bark has proved a useful source. Many natural vegetable dyes are obtained from the bark of trees. Settlers in North America, a heavily forested area, discovered a wealth of dyes in the barks of trees. From Native Americans they learned to produce a brown dye from butternut (*Juglans cinerea*) or white walnut bark. This dye became popular in homespun wool and was also used later for the uniforms of the Confederate army. Other brown dyes come from the alder (*Alnus* sp.), the hemlock (*Tsuga canadensis*), and the red maple (*Acer rubrum*), while yellowish tan dyes come from the bark of the apple (*Malus*), chittan (*Rhamnus purshiana,* also the source of cascara), and the yellow birch (*Betula alleghaniensis*).

The bark of *Corynanthe johimbe* from Cameroon, Africa, has long been touted as an aphrodisiac, but, like most other reputed aphrodisiacs, skeptical pharmacologists and physicians have dismissed it as an old wives' tale. In late 1985, however, scientists John Clark, Erla Smith, and Julian Davidson of Stanford University published an interesting paper in *Science,* showing that yohimbine, one of the alkaloids in *Corynanthe* bark, inhibited the nerve-transmitter hormone, noradrenaline. Sexually experienced male rats injected with yohimbine were twice as ready to mate as untreated ones. Furthermore, virgin male rats, who are often quite shy of mating, also became exceptionally interested in mating when treated with yohimbine and mated a lot sooner than normally expected. They were still interested a week later! The researchers concluded that yohimbine may be an aphrodisiac in humans as well. Would-be experimenters should be cautious because yohimbine interacts with several medications, such as clonidine, and therefore should be treated with respect. Nevertheless, it is interesting that scientists have found substantiation for yet another plant used in indigenous folk culture.

The inner fibrous bark of many trees is used for rope. The Amazon Indians know from which trees bark can be peeled off in a long fibrous strip. Such barks, termed *envira* in Amazonian Brazil, furnish ropes for wrapping cargoes, for shoulder straps, for slings to carry babies, or for lashing a house frame together. Many members of Annonaceae (the *Annona*, or soursop family) or Lecythidaceae (the Brazil nut family) have such barks. *Annona* species have long been used as a source of fiber for cordage, although they have not been used commercially. In the Malay Peninsula, *Anaxagorea javanica* bark is twisted into twine, and in Sulawesi, Indonesia, the bark of *Cananga odorata* is beaten into ropes. In the Sudan in Africa *Hexalobus monopetalus,* an annona, is used for cordage.

The well-known baobab tree (*Adansonia digitata*) of Africa has numerous uses, but many Africans consider its bark the most useful part of the tree. An exceptionally strong and durable fiber is obtained by stripping, pounding, and then soaking the fibers of the inner bark in water. The fibers are used for ropes, fishing nets, sacks, and, in parts of West Africa, are woven into a coarse material for clothing. The fiber is so strong as to give rise to a common Swahili saying: "As secure as an elephant bound with baobab rope."

In Senegal and Ethiopia, baobab fibers are woven into waterproof hats that double as drinking vessels! The outer bark contains a white semifluid gum which oozes from wounds. The gum is odorless and tasteless and is sometimes used to cleanse sores. In Malawi, the flesh of an animal killed by a poisoned arrow has the juice of the bark poured into the arrow wound to neutralize the poison. Baobab bark shares a remarkable feature with cork bark: it is able to replace itself once it has been stripped away. A tree may be girdled from the ground to 8 feet (2.4 meters) above, and the resilient baobab will grow another bark to cover the wound. This is perhaps an adaptation to the attacks of elephants which feed on the baobab bark and wood.

In Peru and Chile, the bark of the soapbox tree (*Quillaja saponaria*) is used as a substitute for soap. The inner bark, which is rich in saponins and forms a lather, is dried and then powdered. It can be used both for washing clothes and as an emulsifying agent in tars. It can also be used as a hair shampoo. In southern Brazil and eastern Argentina, a related tree, *Quillaja brasiliensis*, is also used as a soap.

Bark is much more than a waste product. In addition to the familiar, principal uses for it, such as for cork, tannins, bark cloth, rubber latex, or resins, human ingenuity has found many uses for bark. When good material is available, people tend to make use of it.

FUTHER READING

Clark, J., E. Smith, and J. Davidson. 1985. *Science* 225:847.

OPPOSITE PAGE: The strawberry tree, *Arbutus unedo*, of southern Europe, is often planted because of the ornamental value of its attractive, shreddy bark.

FIBER, FUEL, MULCH, AND OTHER USES OF BARK

ABOVE: An Ojibway lodge. The top half of the lodge is covered with birch bark; the walls are covered with elm bark. Photo © Judith Schmidt.

OPPOSITE PAGE: An Algonquin birch bark tepee being constructed for a museum in Ottawa, Canada. Photo © Judith Schmidt.

FIBER, FUEL, MULCH, AND OTHER USES OF BARK

ABOVE: A house in Australia made from the bark of *Eucalyptus macrorhyncha*, the red stringybark tree. Bark from this species is also used for bark paintings.

OPPOSITE PAGE: A Montagnais birch bark container. The design has been scraped on, revealing the sap. Photo © Judith Schmidt.

FIBER, FUEL, MULCH, AND OTHER USES OF BARK

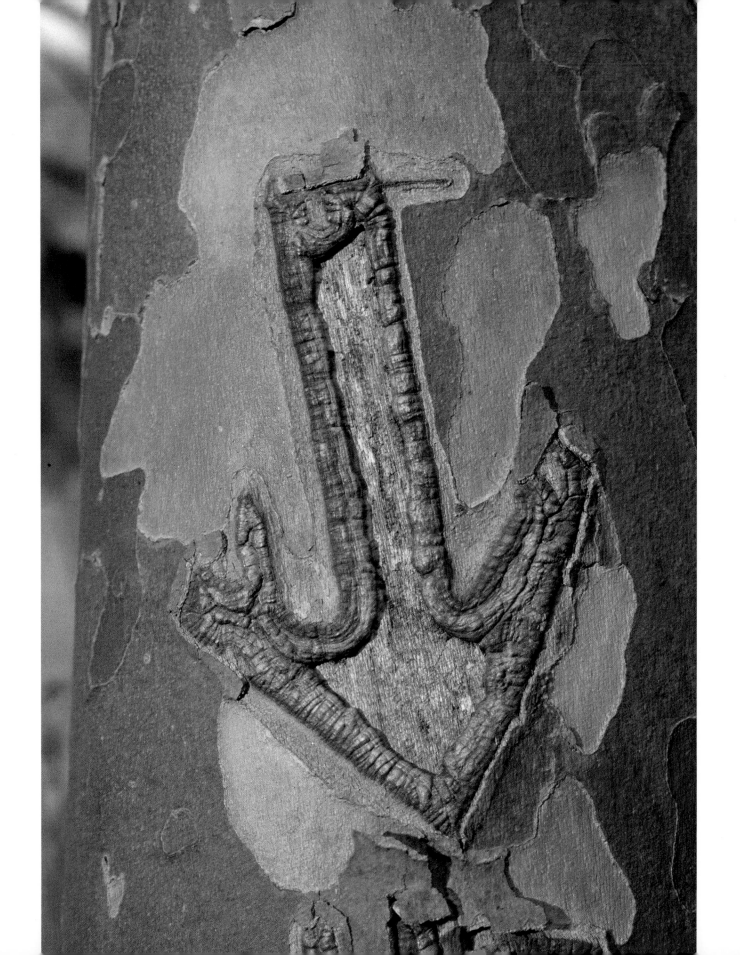

ABOVE: The smooth, light gray bark of the American beech tree, *Fagus grandiflora*, has long been a favorite for graffiti writers.

RIGHT: Fibrous-barked trees are commonly seen in the Amazon forests with their bark stripped off. The bark of this Brazil nut tree has been removed for its ropelike fiber. Photo © G. T. Prance.

OPPOSITE PAGE: Native Americans once marked trails by carving into bark, as here in Sycamore Tree Indian Path, Potomac River, Washington, D.C.

FIBER. FUEL. MULCH. AND OTHER USES OF BARK

• • • • • • • • • • • •

CHAPTER 15

Bark as Camouflage and Food

As anthropocentric creatures, we generally think of bark's usefulness to humans. However, bark is useful to many animals and insects as well. Apart from numerous insects that live in tree bark, many use the exterior of bark as a nesting place simply because they blend so perfectly with it. For these creatures, bark is nature's camouflage.

There is a constant battle between predator and prey in nature. In earlier chapters we saw that bark has an array of chemicals in it to defend the tree from predators, and that often these substances have made various barks useful as a source of medicines, flavors, resins, rubber, and many other products. Some animals and some plants have adopted another strategy to avoid predation. This strategy is camouflage. In any forest there is a large total surface of dappled brown-gray bark, so it is not surprising that a vast array of animals, such as geckos, moths, and beetles, have come to resemble tree bark. By disguising their presence, they avoid being eaten by another animal and thus survive.

Insects that are camouflaged to look like bark usually rest on the tree trunks during the day, and move about to feed and perform their other activities under the cover of darkness. This explains why many nocturnal moths are well camouflaged but many butterflies are not. Butterflies tend to have brighter colors and instead of camouflage they often have chemical defenses. Many butterflies are foul tasting to birds; others mimic these unpalatable butterflies, so that they, too, escape predation. On the other hand, camouflaged insects tend to be palatable to predators; thus their defense depends on camouflage not chemistry. There are insects that match bark, twigs, leaves, stems, flowers, and other common objects in their surroundings. Judging by the number of insects that depend on camouflage for their survival, camouflage is a highly successful strategy.

The peppered moth (*Biston betularia*) of Britain and Europe is an example of the importance of camouflage and the evolution of adaptations toward better disguise. At the beginning of the nineteenth century, this moth typically had pale-colored wings that were speckled black, as if dusted with pepper (hence the name), so that it blended perfectly with lichen-covered tree trunks. Through a rare mutation, occasional individuals had black wings; when resting on a tree, they were very obvious and thus were quickly eaten by predatory birds. However, the nineteenth century brought the industrial revolution and with it considerable pollution in the urban areas of the Midlands of England. Lichens, which are very sensitive to pollution, began to disappear from the trees whose trunks now become blackened by soot. The normal light-colored peppered moths now began to stand out on the black bark, and the rare black individuals became the better adapted variety as now they were camouflaged. Starting with a few survivors, they began to predominate in comparison with their white relatives who were easily visible in the trees and were eaten by birds. By the turn of the century, in industrial areas such as Stoke or Derby, 98 percent of the peppered moths on trees had black wings. Interestingly, in rural areas away from the smoke stacks of central England, the white variety of peppered moth still predominates because it is better camouflaged for the bark of these unpolluted areas.

In North America, a counterpart species, *Biston cognataria,* has undergone similar changes. At least 14 species of underwing moths (*Catocala*) have also become darker in polluted areas where lichens have disappeared from trees. Both the North American and the European species are perfect examples of the principle of "survival of the fittest."

Today, industry is more aware of pollution and much is being done to control it. In some parts of England where pollution has been reduced, lichens are returning to the bark, and along with them, the pale variety of the peppered moth. British geneticist C. A. Clarke and collaborators at the University of Liverpool studied peppered moth populations in West Kirby, England, from 1959 to 1984. During that period, the pale form increased from 6 to 30 percent, apparently due to the decrease of pollution and the return of lichens to tree bark.

Evolution can reverse itself when the environmental cause for the selection of a particular characteristic is reversed.

Moths that rest on tree bark have features other than color to help them hide from predators. For example, when an object is elevated above a flat surface, even if it is well camouflaged, shadows can give it away when the sun is low. Moths eliminate shadow by holding their wings flat against the tree trunk. The edges touch the bark, leaving no gap between the bark and the wing, and slope up from the margin of the wing to the body of the moth is gradual, so no shadow is cast.

Other animals have gone to elaborate means to dispel the giveaway shadow. The flying gecko of Malaysia is so-called because of the wide flap of skin around the edges of its body and tail. Earlier, scientists assumed this flap helped the gecko glide, and so it was named the flying gecko. In fact, the flap, which curls underneath the gecko's body when it is at rest, performs the same function as the moth wings. It breaks up the contour of the animal to reduce shadow.

There is much conjecture about how an animal knows instinctively to rest on an object of the correct color. How does a moth chose a bark that matches its design? From laboratory experiments, scientists know that moths definitely exhibit such a selection, but they still cannot explain the mystery. Scientists have let moths free in large boxes painted with black and white lines. As the moths come to rest at dawn, most white ones choose the white background for their resting place, while darker moths choose the black area in much greater numbers. Although not every insect was perfectly matched to the correct background, a very high percentage chose to rest where they would be less conspicuous. One theory is that a moth is able to match its own reflection with that of the background upon which it lands, but so far this is only one of the many untested theories.

In addition to camouflage, many animals depend on bark for their subsistence. This is obvious to anyone who lives in an area inhabited by deer, rabbits, voles, and other bark-eating animals. Orchardists have a hard time protecting their trees during winter when bark is one of the few sources of food available to rabbits, deer, and other animals. It is obvious that bark is at least a tolerable form of food for these creatures. While bark is an emergency food supply for some animals to carry them through the winter, there are other animals that are much more dependent on bark. Beavers are a good example. Their survival depends on aspen bark. Much of their industrious cutting down of trees is not to build dams, but rather to store aspen bark from the branches for the winter. In search of bark, a beaver may fell 100 trees a year!

Sapsucker woodpeckers drill small evenly spaced rows of holes into the inner bark of trees. They drink the sap of the tree from these wells and also feed on insects that are caught in the sticky sap. If they are too active on a particular tree, they may kill it.

A fascinating method of sustenance has developed in various

species of South American marmosets. The common marmoset (*Callithrix jacchus penicillata*) of central Brazil is a good example. These small monkeys gnaw tiny holes in the bark of certain tree species to obtain the exuding sap for food. Marmosets are known to use fourteen species of trees, but apparently prefer three common ones. They visit the holes regularly to feed on the sap and gum which flow from the holes. These saps and gums are rich in sugars and micronutrients, which are important in the marmosets' diets, especially at times when fruits are scarce. Only a few species of the South American primates in the genera *Callithrix* and *Cebuella* are adapted to feeding from tree sap, but for these species sap constitutes a large proportion of their diet.

The tropical squirrel *Sundasciurus lowii* lives on the small island of Siberut in Indonesia, where its diet consists almost entirely of tree bark. The Sunda squirrel is not as destructive as the common gray squirrel of North America and Great Britain which strips large areas of bark and often kills the tree; the Sunda squirrel removes only small flakes of bark, even from trees whose bark is easy to strip, and so it does not destroy its food source. None of the food trees this squirrel feeds on produce sap, and so unlike the marmoset, it feeds on the bark itself rather than on the bark exudates.

Like humans, animals have adapted so that they, too, are users of bark. Next time you walk in a forest, look closely at the tree trunks for camouflaged insects. Often they are extremely difficult to spot because their camouflage is so perfect.

FURTHER READING

Bishop, J. A., and L. M. Cook. 1975. "Moth, Melanism and Clean Air." *Scientific American* 232:90–99.

Kettlewell, B. 1973. *The Evolution of Melanism.* Oxford: Clarendon Press.

Leibert, T. G., and P. M. Brakefield. 1987. "Behavioural Studies in the Peppered Moth *Biston betularia* and a Discussion of the Role of the Pollution and Lichens in Industrial Melanism." *Biological Journal of the Linnean Society* 31:129–150.

OPPOSITE PAGE, TOP: *Calypteris idomea* from Venezuela is a member of Noctuidae, a large family of moths.

OPPOSITE PAGE, BOTTOM: *Perigea stelligera,* a Noctuidae from Venezuela.

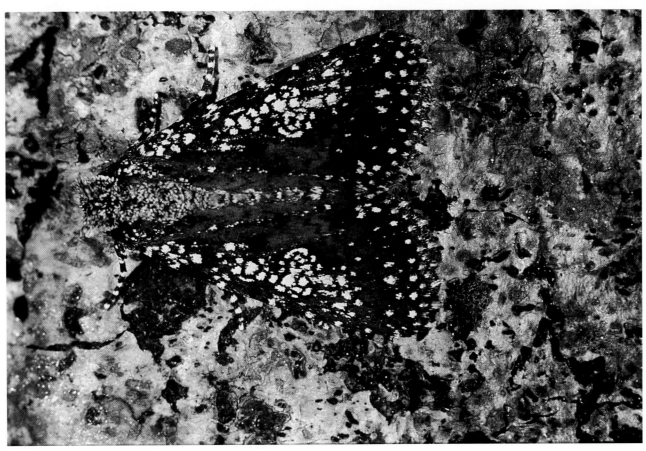

ABOVE: This *Euglyphis* moth from Amazonas, Brazil, is a member of Lasiocampidae, a family of tan or grayish moths.

TOP RIGHT: *Plutodes discigera*, a Geometridae moth from New Guinea.

MIDDLE RIGHT: This *Hemistola* moth fron Trinidad is a member of Geometridae.

BOTTOM RIGHT: A tiger moth of Geometridae from Malaya.

RIGHT: This *Euglyphis* species from Costa Rica is a member of Lasiocampidae.

BELOW: This *Melese* moth from Venezuela is a member of the Arctiidae.

BARK AS CAMOUFLAGE AND FOOD

LEFT: *Blocynis xylia* from Venezuela is a member of the Noctuidae.

OPPOSITE PAGE: *Platysenta apameoides*. Noctuidae moth from Venezuela, has false eye spots.

BARK AS CAMOUFLAGE AND FOOD

OPPOSITE PAGE: The hawk moth, *Amplypterus gannascus,* from Manaus, Brazil, is a member of the Sphingidea.

BELOW: A *Hemidactylus* lizard on bark in Rio de Janeiro, Brazil.

BELOW: A large katydid blends in with bark at Auaris, Brazil. Photo © G. T. Prance.

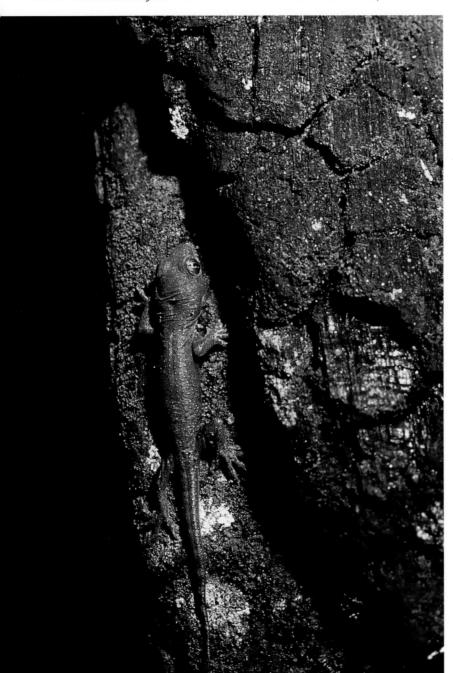

OPPOSITE PAGE: The gliding gecko, *Ptychozoon kuhlii*, well disguised on bark in Sumatra.

BELOW: The ant's nest beetle, *Paussus cucullatus*, from South Africa is a member of Pausidae.

BELOW: Fungus beetles, *Eumorphus*, of the Endomychidae on bark in Sri Lanka.

BARK AS CAMOUFLAGE AND FOOD

ABOVE: A tree frog, *Hyla pardalis*, on bark in Rio de Janeiro, Brazil.

RIGHT: Beavers fell many aspen (*Populus*) trees to obtain bark, their principal food source. Photo © G. T. Prance.

OPPOSITE PAGE: A Dobson fly, *Corydalus,* in Manaus, Brazil, is a good match for the bark of this tree.

BARK AS CAMOUFLAGE AND FOOD

CHAPTER 16

Bark Flora

The patterns and colors on the bark of many trees are not part of the bark itself, but come from the lichens which grow on it. These lichens often form a crustlike cover over the bark to give the tree trunk a patchy appearance and add color to the forest. Lichens are unusual, since they are a combination of two plants—an alga and a fungus—which grow together in a symbiotic relationship and form a new plant, the lichen. They have adapted to many harsh environments in the world where other plants cannot grow, such as on rocks or tree trunks. Bark lichens are described as *corticolous*, from the Latin word for bark, *cortex*. Similarly, lichens that grow on leaves are described as *foliicolous*. The algal part of the lichen contains chlorophyll and enables the plant to absorb the sun's energy and manufacture sugars through the process of photosynthesis. The fungal part uses food from the algal cells, and in return, absorbs water and nutrients from the substrate upon which they grow.

Lichens are the main food of caribou and reindeer which eat from 6 to 10 pounds (2.7 to 4.5 kilograms) of lichens a day. These animals eat lichens which grow on the ground and are therefore easy to browse. When the ground is frozen, the Lapps and the Eskimos cut down lichen-laden trees to provide fodder for reindeer. The lichens which provide food for reindeer are not crusts growing flat against the trunk, but have the branched, more leaflike structure of leafy, or foliose, lichens. The lichens that ornament bark are principally of two types: foliose or crustose.

In some cities around the world, lichens no longer decorate tree trunks. They are extremely sensitive to air pollution and have disappeared as a result of the pollutants in the air. Recently, the presence or absence of lichens on trees has been a useful indicator of the degree of pollution in the area. This, however, is no new discovery. As early as 1866, French scientist W. Nylander suggested that the absence of lichens in the outskirts of the Jardins de Luxembourg in Paris was due to air pollution from the surrounding buildings. Lichens are particularly sensitive to sulfur dioxide, one of the most common industrial pollutants. This has caused lichen deserts in many of our industrial areas. The lichen *Licanora conizoides* is most resistant to sulfur dioxide and has, therefore, replaced all other lichens in many urban areas. Its presence is a good indicator of pollution.

Because lichens are a mixture of two organisms (the alga and the fungus), plants of the same species do not consistently grow in the same fashion, and, so unlike other plants, they cannot always be identified by their appearance. In the case of bark lichens, the texture and hardness of the bark can determine the form lichens take. A species of lichen can have one external appearance on the smooth twigs of an ash tree and another quite different appearance on the rougher-barked older branches of the same tree. Since lichen form is so varied, taxonomists, who classify the various species, resort to chemistry to identify the species rather than rely on external morphology alone.

The external form of a lichen species is often modified by the properties of the substrate upon which it grows. For example, the well-named bark lichen *Graphis scripta* grows in elongated strands as a result of its apothecium which follows the wood grain.

The variation in the pH of bark affects the lichen flora on the tree. For example, many oak and pine trees have highly acidic bark and are consequently not good substrates for lichens. Perhaps acid bark protects them from an excess of lichens. The white oak (*Quercus alba*), however, has a less acidic bark and as a result has a large lichen flora.

If you examine many trees with lichens on the bark, you will discover patterns that indicate their distribution on the bark is not random. One of the most imporant influences of spatial distribution is the availability of moisture from rainfall, dew, or stem flow. Lichens need water and the nutrients that it contains. The availability of light also affects the position of lichens on a tree trunk.

Some lichens, especially crustose ones, penetrate deeply into the corky layers of the bark, while others, such as many foliose lichens, are anchored shallowly onto the bark. Some lichens grow into the nutrient-rich inner bark, the cambium, or even under wood cells of a tree trunk, to obtain nourishment. As a result of this direct growth into the bark, lichens can cause bark to break up. Lichens can also be a burden to the tree because they trap pockets of moisture that are ideal habitats for fungi. Many species of insects live in or under lichens and use these areas to infest and damage the tree. Thus, although lichens add to the variety and beauty of bark, they can also cause considerable damage to the tree. Some trees defend against lichens with flaky bark. A bark that consistently flakes discards the burden of the lichens and protects the tree.

Lichens are dispersed by minute seedlike diaspores which must attach themselves to the substrate on which they grow. The diaspores are trapped much more easily on a rough surface than on a smooth one. Consequently, lichens are more abundant on rough-barked trees that are not too flaky, and many smooth-barked trunks bear no lichens at all. There are a few crustose lichens, however, that have specialized in the colonization of smooth-barked trees. One example is the lichen *Pyrenula nitidella* which grows only on the smooth-barked beech trunk.

Some tree trunks appear to have very consistent lichen patterns. The reason for this is that some lichens are highly specific to a particular species of tree. This is particularly true of the crustose lichens and less true of the foliose ones. For example, the lichen *Conotrema urceolatum* is restricted to the sugar maple (*Acer saccharum*) and *Calicium curtissii* to the sumac species *Rhus typhina*. The lichen *Parmeliopsis placardia* is specific to pitch pine (*Pinus rigida*) on the East Coast of North America, the jack pine (*Pinus banksiana*) in the Great Lakes region, and the ponderosa pine (*Pinus ponderosa*) on the West Coast.

Tropical forests are renowned for their diversity of tree species. They also have a richer bark-lichen flora than their temperate-region counterparts. The trunks of many tropical rainforest trees are a mosaic of species-rich lichen communities with one species blending into another.

Lichens are usually the first plants to colonize a tree trunk, but once there, they open the way for many other plants to colonize the tree, especially in tropical forests where a variety of mosses and liverworts ornament the tree trunks. These plants establish in the damp places and cracks caused by the growth of lichens. There are even some minute ferns and seed plants that are found on tree trunks. Some of the most common bark plants are various species of *Peperomia* in the black pepper family. Once a colony of lichens and mosses is established on a tree trunk, enough moisture is retained for the peperomias, various orchids, and ferns also grow on the trunk.

The trunks of many tropical trees support a diverse flora of lichens, mosses, liverworts, and a few flowering plants, but the branches of the same trees may have an even more spectacular flora because they are often laden with air plants or epiphytes. Epiphytes are plants that perch on other plants; they are not parasites because they do not take nutrients from their host. Most epiphytes, such as many orchids, aroids, and bromeliads which have become familiar house plants, grow naturally on the branches of trees, but a few also grow on the trunk. Their presence depends on the chemistry of the bark, and, as with lichens, rough-barked trees tend to have many more epiphytes than smooth-barked ones. That is because it is easier for the seeds, which have been carried to the branches either by wind, as in the case of the dustlike orchids seeds, or by birds, to establish on a rough bark.

The result is that the tree branches of many tropical forests are laden with epiphytes, which can become a burden to the trees and cause the branches to break. Some trees, however, have adapted to this situation by putting out roots, from their branches, into the soil that accumulates around the base of the epiphytes. This soil accumulates around the roots of the epiphyte, especially when various insects such as ants make their home there. Putting out branch roots is one way some trees are able to take advantage of the burden which they bear. Nutrients are so scarce in the tropical rain forest that none can be wasted and all are recycled rapidly.

ABOVE: Lichens on the shady side of a royal palm, *Roystonea,* in Miami, Florida.

ABOVE: Lichens decorate the trunk of *Strombosia zeylanica* in Ceylon.

ABOVE: Lichens on the trunk of *Cecropia peltata*, the trumpet tree, from Jamaica, give this species its patchy appearance.

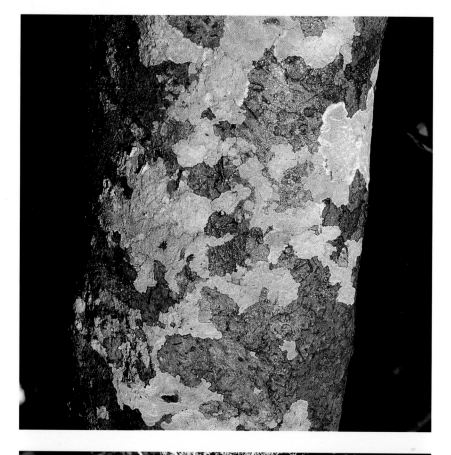

ABOVE: Lichens on the trunk of an *Astrocaryum mexicanum* palm in Panama.

TOP LEFT: Lichens on the bark of a *Eugenia* tree in Sumatra.

BOTTOM LEFT: Lichens on the trunk of a cinnamon tree, *Cinnamomum ovalifolium*, in Sri Lanka.

OPPOSITE PAGE: Lichens and liverworts on the trunk of the red silk-cotton tree, *Bombax malabaricum*, in Indochina.

BARK FLORA

ABOVE: Trunk of *Araucaria hunstenii* from Australia with young leaves.

LEFT: A wild *Dendrobium macrophyllum* orchid growing on a trunk in New Guinea.

BARK FLORA

ABOVE: Orchid roots forming a network on a tree trunk near the Amazon River, Leticia, Columbia.

ABOVE: Epiphytic plants and lichens cover the trunk of a *Symplocos furcata* tree.

TOP LEFT: Moss growing on a tree trunk in a rain forest in Sri Lanka.

BOTTOM LEFT: Fungus on branch in rain forest of New Guinea.

BELOW: Some trees produce flowers out of the trunk, as does this *Swartzia* from Manaus, Brazil.

OPPOSITE PAGE: A *Marasmius* fungus in the Peruvian rain forest near Tingo Maria.

BARK FLORA

BARK FLORA

The Sachimanga tree or *Grias* from Brazil produces flowers from the trunk, which, in this photograph, are being visited by a *Helicopis acis* butterfly.

TOP RIGHT: A young vine creeps up the trunk of *Parkia roxburghiana* in Malaya.

BOTTOM RIGHT: Epiphytes, including *Ficus diversiformis*. the creeping fig, growing on a trunk in Sri Lanka.

BELOW: A red silk-cotton tree, *Bombax malabaricum*, laden with epiphytes or air plants.

BARK FLORA

ABOVE: *Ficus parcellii*, a strangler fig, envelopes its host with a network of joined stems in the Florida Everglades.

RIGHT: Strangler fig trees, such as this one in Sri Lanka, often begin as epiphytes, wrapping their roots around the host.

BARK FLORA

LEFT: Strangler fig trees, like this one in Wau, New Guinea, eventually strangle their hosts and become established in their own right.

BELOW: *Ficus leprieuri* from Ghana with strangled host.

• • • • • • • • • • • • •

Bark Dwellers

The bark of some trees, especially old and partially decayed trees, is a veritable zoo. Beetles, termites, moth larvae, lizards, and frogs inhabit various barks.

Tree frogs are most abundant in the tropical forest where they have no need for shelter from the cold. The North American gray tree frog (*Hyla versicolor*), however, must find somewhere to overwinter. These frogs, which live in low trees and shrubs in the eastern United States, pass the winter under the bark of trees. Research has shown that they are one of the few species of frog with the capacity to regenerate lost limbs. Unfortunately for the frogs, this means that studies are underway to develop a market for the legs of this species!

Another animal which overwinters in tree bark is the mourning cloak butterfly. The adult form passes the winter under the bark of the sugar maple (*Acer saccharum*) and emerges during the early spring thaw when it can be seen fluttering around trunk scars which run with the sugar rich sap.

A well-known tree in the hills around Canberra, Australia, is the scribbly gum, so named because of the weird-looking hieroglyphics on the pale-colored bark of the tree. The markings on the bark are due to the larvae of the scribbly gum moth, aptly named *Ogmograptis scribula*. The adult moths lay their eggs between the new and the old year's bark layers. When the larvae hatch, they burrow between the bark layers to feed and thus leave a wandering tunnel, which is visible when the old bark falls away. As the larvae gradually increase in size, the tunnels also progressively increase in size. Since the larvae never seem to bore their passages in a straight line, they doodle all over the tree trunk in such a way that it is not surprising that this thin-barked eucalyptus species is known as the scribbly gum tree.

The most common and most important bark dwellers are the bark or engraver beetles, members of the beetle family, Scolytidae, whose name literally means tree cutters. Some scolytids live in wood and are known as ambrosia beetles while others, the bark beetles, live in bark. While bark beetles generally feed on the inner bark and cause considerable damage to the tree, their relatives, the ambrosia beetles, feed on fungal material that grows in the tree. They are, nonetheless, considerable pests because they cause damage to the wood.

A familiar site on an old tree branch or fallen trunk that has lost its bark is the characteristic patterns carved in the inner bark and outer wood by bark beetles. The intricacy and variety of such patterns far exceeds that of the scribbly gum moth. Many bark beetles carve out distinctively shaped or branched tunnels by which the species can be identified. Tunnels may be simple and cavelike, elaborate star-shaped, simple forked, or many-branched structures.

Bark beetles themselves do not cause serious damage to the trees. Their main danger, which makes them a serious pest, is that they either spread tree disease or open cavities into the bark which are easily infected by fungal disease. The beetle galleries permit the entrance of fungi which can then rot the bark and even the wood.

Perhaps the best known and most feared of all bark beetles is the elm bark beetle, *Scolytus multistriatus*. It is the chief vector of Dutch elm disease that has killed the majestic elm trees of Europe and North America. The disease is a fungus that is spread by the beetles as they mine into the bark. It did not occur in North America until, unfortunately, it was introduced from Europe by the timber trade, hence the Dutch got blamed for the disease! Few elm trees remain, except in isolated areas where the beetles have not reached them. For that reason some of the best examples of the American elm are to be found in Central Park in the middle of New York City.

Bark beetles are small robust or slender insects with, according to beetle specialists, relatively primitive mouth parts well adapted for biting and chewing wood. Both the larvae and the adult stages have these well-developed mandibles which enable them to chew and penetrate almost any type of material.

The beetles enter the bark at leaf scars, crevices, or through other irregularities in the bark. They usually bore into the bark obliquely upwards for two reasons: (1) the hole is thus protected from rainfall and stem-flow water, and (2) it facilitates the removal of frass in a downwards direction.

Bark beetles are one of the few insects in which the adult burrows into the host plant to deposit its eggs directly into the food material of the larvae. Most insects have elaborate egg-laying devices to insert the eggs into the larval food plants. The presence of the adult beetles in the tunnels offers protection to the larvae. The adult beetles remain in the galleries to prevent attacks by predators or the entry of various parasites. They are well protected in the concealed tunnels within the bark. However, both the adult bark beetles and their larvae are a favorite food of various species of woodpeckers.

Another feature of bark beetles is their tolerance to adverse environments. They are tolerant of extreme temperatures and they are also unharmed by many substances that are toxic to other insects. This makes the bark beetles widespread and hard to control so that several species are regarded as serious pests of the timber and orchard industries. Because bark beetles are unharmed by conifer resin or by resin vapor, they are pests of many cone-bearing trees. They are able to overcome the plant's defense system and thus live in the bark of these resin-bearing trees. For example, many species of the beetle genus *Dendroctonus* (the name means killer of trees) are listed as pests of national importance because they inhabit trees of considerable value. The noxious beetles include southern and western pine beetle. As their names indicate, many beetle species are specific to a certain tree and maybe its nearest relatives. The pine engravers, such as the aptly named California pine engraver, *Ips plastographus*, are listed as pests. Since the family of bark beetles, the Scolytidae, contains 625 species placed in 73 different genera, they have a fearful potential to injure tree bark and wood!

Between 1950 and 1955 there was a great surge in the population of the great spruce bark beetle (*Dendroctonus micans*) in Denmark. Entomologist Bejer Petersen studied this pest which attacked both spruce and Scotch pine. The adult beetles eat out a round chamber which is less than 1 inch (2.5 centimeters) in diameter, and lay the eggs in small heaps against the walls of this cavity. The female produces from 100 to 200 eggs. After a month, the eggs hatch and the larvae begin to feed communally at the margin of the brood chamber which they enlarge and fill with frass. Later, the larvae pupate in the mass of light brown frass and overwinter before emerging as adult beetles to disperse to a new tree.

The dispersal phase of bark beetles reveals another of their well-developed characteristics, namely, a sophisticated chemical communication system. These beetles can sense other host trees, especially when the trees are injured and emit an odor from resins, terpenes, and other volatile compounds. Once a beetle has found a host tree, it can attract a mate by emitting scents or pheromones. In the wood engravers (*Ips*), the male beetles disperse to the new trees, whereas in the bark beetles (*Dendroctonus*), the females disperse and then attract a mate. Once they have established themselves with a mate on a new tree, it is not in their interest to attract more insects to compete with them for food, and so they release repellant hormones.

Bark beetles communicate in another way that is unusual for beetles but common in other insects such as crickets: they produce a sound by friction, which is called *stridulation*. These noises are apparently produced from inside their bark chambers to warn off neighbors. Even so, in heavy infestations of bark beetles, the cavities can be so dense they merge.

One of the most feared pests among the bark beetles is the shot hole borer or fruit-tree bark beetle, *Scolytus rugulosus*. It attacks the lower 6 feet (1.8 meters) of many useful orchard trees, including almond, apple, apricot, cherry, loquat, peach, plum, and quince. It prejudices and reduces the crop by disturbing the water economy of the trees, which in turn causes considerable damage to the inner bark. The host hole borer is another pest of European origin that was introduced into North America. It is easy to understand why there are strict controls on the importation of plant and animal material from one country to another; restrictions discourage the introduction of further noxious pests such as the elm bark beetle and the shot hole borer.

Home dwellers in North America dread termites because they can invade a house and quickly eat away the woodwork. In tropical rain forests, termites abound and can be seen on the trunks of almost any tree. However, they are actually less destructive than the bark beetles. Hardly any species of termite attacks living wood; instead, they assist with the rapid destruction and recycling of dead wood and thus play a useful role in the tropical forest life cycle.

Termite nests occur on the ground in mounds several feet tall, or as large masses near the top of the trees, or as carefully built structures flat against tree trunks. Many termite nests that are higher up a tree are connected to the ground by a long tunnel, which is laboriously built from mud to protect these rather fragile insects as they move from their nest to forage in the forest.

Termite nests that are built on tree bark are most interesting because of their structure. They are usually strategically placed on a trunk in the area that receives the least stem flow water. On a wet day, frequently the nest is on the only dry part of the trunk. Other nests on tree trunks are built with a series of tunnels that channel the water away from the nest. These tunnels often make use of the natural features of the bark such as its fissures. Thus, they blend well with the bark and are difficult to see. These insects engineer a nest in such a way as to control water flow, just as we channel water from the roofs of our houses through a system of gutters and downpipes.

Bark is an abundant resource in any forest, and because of its great variety, it is not surprising that a vast number of insects and other animals have made it their home.

ABOVE: These characteristic marks in the bark of the scribbly gum tree, *Eucalyptus rossii*, are made by the larva of the scribbly gum moth. As the larva grows, the width of the channel increases.

ABOVE: Worm in the bark of a clove tree in the Molucca Islands.

ABOVE: A cerambycid wood boring beetle from New Guinea.

OPPOSITE PAGE: A buprestid beetle, *Enchroma gigantes,* on the kapok tree, *Ceiba pentandra,* in Brazil.

BARK DWELLERS

ABOVE: Termite tracks on a New Caledonia pine, *Araucaria cookii.*

RIGHT: Termite tunnels and exuded resin on a tree in the Ghanaian rain forest.

OPPOSITE PAGE: Termite nest on a tree in Ghana.

ABOVE: A termite nest on a tree trunk near Manaus, Brazil. The nest is built in such a way as to channel the rain water flowing down the trunk away from the nest. Photo © G. T. Prance.

RIGHT: Snails on the trunk of a *Gyrostemon ramulosus* tree in Perth, Australia.

OPPOSITE PAGE: A toad, *Bufo marinus*, feeding on black wasps in Panama.

170

INDEX OF SCIENTIFIC NAMES

Abuta 74
Acacia 92
  decurrens 92
  nilotica 92
Acer griseum 125
  nigrum 118
  rubrum 125
  saccharum 118, 149, 162
Achras sapota 57
Adansonia digitata 126
Agathis 63
  dammara 15, 66
  robusta 18
Alnus 125
Amplypterus gannascus 142
Anaxogorea javanica 126
Annona glabra 98
Annonaceae 33, 126
Antiaris toxicaria 76, 115
Antonia ovata 49
Apocynaceae 57
Arapaima gigas 33
Araucaria
  cookii 168
  hunstenii 154
Arbutus unedo 44, 125, 127
Arctiidae 139
Aristolochia 24
Artocarpus 104
  altissima 35
Asclepias 56
Astrocaryum mexicanum 53, 152
Azadirachta indica 52

Bactris 51
Banisteriopsis caapi 79, 80
  inebrians 79
  rusbyana 80
Betula 92, 95
  alleghaniensis 125
  occidentalis 14
  papyrifera 118, 121
Biston betularia 135
  cognataria 135
Bixa orellana 102, 104
Blocynis xylia 140
Bombacaceae 39
Bombax malabaricum 44, 53, 153, 159
Boswellia 63
  carteri 63
Brachychiton rupestris 39
Brosimum parinarioides 33
Broussonetia papyrifera 104, 115
Bufo marinus 171
Bursera simaruba 19, 39, 41, 46, 65
Burseraceae 63

Caesalpinia ferrea 26
Calicium curtisii 149
Callithrix 136
  jacchus penicillata 136
Calycophyllum 33
Calypteris idomea 137
Cananga odorata 126
Carya 117
  ovata 23, 34
Caryocar glabrum 75
Castanea dentata 92, 117
Castilla 56, 57
Catocala 135
Cebuella 136
Cecropia peltata 151
Ceiba pentandra 167
Ceridium praecox 39
  torreyanum 39
Chondrodendron 74
Chrysobalanaceae 34
Cinchona 73
  ledgeriana 73
Cinnamomum camphora 31, 87
  cassia 85
  ovalifolum 152
  verum 88
  zeylanicum 84
Citrus limon 15
Colubrina 86
  arborescens 89
  elliptica 86, 89
Commiphora 64
  opobulsam 63
Conotrema urceolatum 149
Copaifera 63
Cornus alba 125
Corydalus 146
Corynanthe johimbe 125
Corythophora rimosa 33
Couepia elata 33
Couma 57
Couratari 33
Curarea 74
  toxicofera 74

Dendroctonus 163
  micans 163
Dipterocarpaceae 63
Dracaena ellenbeckiana 21
Duguetia latifolia 74

Enchroma gigantes 167
Endomychidae 145
Enterolobium cyclocarpum 28
Eriodendron anfractuosum 45, 51
Eschweilera odora 33
Euphorbiaceae 33, 56
Eucalpytus 16, 36, 49
  citriodora 18, 50

deglupta 40, 41
macrorhyncha 130
nudiniana 42, 43
pauciflora 22
pauciflora subsp.
  niphophila 17
rossii 165
rubida 29
viminalis 61
Eugenia 152
Euglyphis 138, 139
Eumorphus 145

Fagus grandifolia 133
Ficus 11
  benjamina 27
  cotinifolia 105
  diversiformis 159
  elastica 21, 36, 60
  leprieuri 161
  padifolia 105
  parcellii 160
  tecolutensis 105

Galipea cusparia 85
Genipa 114
Geometridae 138
Gliricidia sepium 60
Goupia glabra 33
Graphis scripta 149
Grias 158
Guarea 74
Guttiferae 33, 35
Gyrostemon ramulosus 53, 170

Hamamelis virginiana 72
Helicopis acis 158
Hemidactylus 143
Hemistola 138
Hevea 26, 33, 56
  brasiliensis 56, 57, 58
Hexalobus monopetalus 126
Hibiscus 104
Humiria 33
Hura crepitans 48
Hyla
  pardalis 147
  versicolor 162
Hymenaea courbaril 33, 63, 119

Ips 163
  plastographus 163

Juglans cinerea 125
Justicia 82

Kalanchoe beharensis 20

Lasio campidea 138, 139
Lauraceae 86
Lecythidaceae 126
Lecythis pisonis 24
Leguminosae 63
Licania 33, 34
  heteromorpha 33
Licanora conizoides 149
Lithocarpus densiflora 92
Lonchocarpus 75

Macrolobium limbatum 33
Malpighiaceae 79
Malus 125
Manihot 779
Manilkara 57
  zapota 60
Marasmius 157
Melaleuca minor 34
  quinquenervia 16
Melese 139
Menispermaceae 74
Microcyclus ulei 57
Moraceae 57, 104
Musanga smithii 98
Myriocarpa longipes 105

Noctuidae 137, 140, 141
Nothfagus betuloides 119

Ocotea pretiosa 86
Ogmograptis scribula 163
Oncospermum horridum 51
Opuntia echios 30

Pachira 39, 111
Pachypodium
  rutenbergianum 40
Pachyrhynchus orbifer 67
Palaquium gutta 577
Parinari obtusifolia 48
Parkia roxburghiana 159
Parkinsonia aculeata 39
Parmeliopsis placordia 149
Parthenium argentata 56
Paullinia cupana 74
  yoco 74
Pausidae 145
Paussus cucullatus 145
Peperomia 149
Pereskia 52
Perigea stelligera 137
Phyllocladus trichomanoides 92
Picea 117
  glauca 118
  mariana 118
Pimenta acris 19, 88
Pinus banksiana 149
  bungeana 125
  canariensis 30

massoniana 68
mercusii 98
ponderosa 149
rigida 149
Pipturus albidus 104
Pistacia lentiscus 64
Platanus × acerifolia 23
Platysenta apameoides 141
Plutodes discigera 138
Podocnemis expansa 75
Populus 117, 147
Protium 64
Prunus maackii 125
Pseudobombax ellipticum 45
  maximum 39
Psychotria psychotriaefolia 80
  viridis 80
Ptychozoon kuhlii 144
Pyrenula nitidella 149

Quercus alba 92, 149
  infectoria 91
  occidentalis 97
  prinus 92
  rubra 92
  suber 96, 99, 101
  velutina 92
Quillaja brasiliensis 126
  saponaria 126

Rhamnus purshiana 72, 125
Rhizophora 92
  mangle 93, 94
Rhoicissus rhomboidea 20
Rhus typhina 149
Roystonea 150
Rubiaceae 72
Rutaceae 48

Salix 92
Samanea saman 21, 69
Sapotaceae 57
Sassafras albidum 85
Scolytidae 163
Scolytus multistriatus 163
  rugulosus 164
Sphingiidae 142
Sterculiaceae 33
Stereospermum kunthianum 45
Strombosia ceylanica 151
Strychnos 74
  solimoesana 74
Styrax 64
Sundascirus lowii 136
Swartzia 156
Symplocos furcata 155

Taraxacum 56
Taxus brevifolia 73

Terminalia bellerica 91
  chebula 91
Theobroma cacao 37
Thuja occidentalis 118

Tilia 117
  americana 118
Trema micrantha 105
Tsuga canadensis 91, 125

heterophylla 91

Ulmus 117
  suberosa 98

Urera baccifera 105
Urticaceae 104

Virola 78, 79, 81, 82

theiodora 78

Zanthoxylum martinicense 48

GENERAL INDEX

Abaanaki Indians 118, 123
Acacia 90
Achiote 102, 104
Adney, Edwin Tappan 117, 118
African wattle 92
Ahu 105
Alacaluf Indians 119
Alder 125
Alexander the Great 73
Alga, as lichen symbiont 149
Algonquin Indians 118, 129
Alkaloids,
  bisbenzylisoquinoline 74
  bisindole 74
Allspice 88
Amahuca Indians 80
Amate 105, 112, 113
Amber 63, 67
Ampá doce 33
Angostura bitters 85
Annona family 33, 74, 126
Apple 125
Arana, Julio C. 57
Araucaria 63, 168
Arecuna Indians 119
Arrow poison 74
Aspen 135, 147
Araucarias 63
Ayahuasca 79, 80
Aztecs 104, 105

Bacteria 26
Balala 74
Balata 57
Balm of Gilead 64
Balsams 26
Banks, Joseph 104
Baobab 126
Bark
  as aphrodisiac 125, 126
  ecology 47–54
  as flavor 84–89
  as food 135, 136
  as fuel 125
  as a hallucinogen 78–83
  houses of 120, 128, 129, 130
  inner 24, 25
  in landscape 125
  as medicine 70–76

outer 24, 25
pH of 149
as poison 73–75
as soap 126
as rope 126
velvet leaf 20
Bark cloth 103–115
Basswood 117, 118
Bast 24, 25
  cloth 103
Bate-Smith, E. C. 91
Bay berry 19, 88
Beaver 135, 147
Beech 133
  southern 119
Beetle
  ambrosia 163
  ant's nest 145
  bark 163
  buprestid 167
  California pine engraver 163
  cerambycid wood-borer 166
  elm bark 163
  engraver 163
  fruit-tree bark 164
  fungus 145
  great spruce bark 163
  shot-hole borer 164
  snout 67
  southern pine 163
  western pine 163
Benzoin 64
Beothul Indians 118
Bicava 74
Birch 24, 92, 95, 124, 128, 129, 131
  paper 117, 121, 122
  water 14
  yellow 125
Birthwort 24
Black pepper family 149
Boa 74
Boehm, R. 74
Bombax family 39, 45
Bora Indians 79, 105, 110
Bounty 105
Branch scar 32
Brazil nut
  family 33, 126

tree 133
Brazilian ironwood 26
Breadfruit 76, 104
Buckthorn, western 72
Bursera family 64
Butterfly 135, 158
  mourning cloak 162
Butternut 125

Caatinga 39
Cacao 37
Cactus 38, 52
  prickly pear 30
Caffeine 74
Calophony 64
Cambium 24, 25
Camouflage 134–147
Camphor tree 31, 87
Canoes 14, 116–123
Canot de maitre 118
Caripe 33
Caripuna Indians 117
Cartier, Jacques 117
Cascara sagrada 72
Cassia 85
Castanha jacaré 33
Catalpa family 45
Caoutchouc 57
Cedar 123
  white 118
Celery grass 119
Cells, conductive 25, 26
  cork 24, 25
  fiber 24
  parenchyma 24
  ray 25, 26
  sieve 24
Chácobo Indians 104
Champlain, Samuel 116, 117
Chapelle, Howard I. 117
Cheira pau 33
Cherry 24
Chestnut, American 92, 117
Chichicastle 105
Chile 119
Chinchon, Countess of 73
Chipboard 125
Chippewa Indians 72
Chittan bark 125
Chlorenchyma 39
Chlorophyll 38

Chono Indians 119
Cinchona 72
Cinnamic aldehyde 85
Cinnamon 14, 84, 85, 152
Cipó 80
Clark, John 125
Clarke, C. A. 135
Clonidine 126
Clove 165
Cocoa family 33
Collagen 91
Columbus, Christopher 56
Condamine, Charles de la 56
Cook, James 104, 105
Copal 33, 62, 63
  Africa 63
  Manila 66
Cordova-Rios, Manuel 80
Coreghaje Indians 74
Cork 24, 96–101
  board 98
  cambium 24, 25
Cortex 25
Cottonwood 117
Cree Indians 118, 119
Cromwell, Oliver 73
Cupiuba tree 33
Curare 74, 77
Curarine 74

Dandelion 55
Davidson, Julian 125
Dobson fly 146
Dogrib Indians 118
Douglas fir 48
Dragon tree 21
Drake, Francis 85
Dunlop, John 56
Dyes 104, 125

Earpod tree 28
Elm 128, 163
  English witch 72
  thick-barked 98
Envira 33, 126
Epidermis 39
Epiphytes 149, 150, 159
Episcopi chronicon 117
Eskimos 148
Espino tree 48
Eucalyptus 16, 18, 36, 40, 41, 49, 50, 130

Farinha seca 33
Fats 26
Feltbush 20
Fiberboard 125
Fig 105
  Benjamin 27
  family 57
  strangling 11, 160, 161
Fire 48
Fish poison 75
Flax 26
Flint, Howard 48
Frankincense 62, 63
Fuegans 119
Fungus 149, 156, 157
  as lichen symbiont 149

Gallotannins 91
Galls 91
Geckos, flying 135
  gliding 144
Genip 114
Gerard, John 85
Girdling 26
Glucosides 91
Goodyear, Charles 56
Gray, Dr. 74
Guaraná plant 74
Guayule 56
Gum
  chewing 55, 57
  tree 40
Gumbo limbo tree 19, 39, 41, 46, 65
Gutta percha 57

Haberlandt, G. 24
Hallucinogenic substances 78–83
Halton, Dr. 74
Harmaline 80
Harmine 80
Hemlock 91, 125
  western 91
Hemp 26
Hiawatha 118
Hickory 117
  shagbark 23, 32, 34
Hibiscus 104
Homstedt, Bo 79
Homburger, F. 85

Hooker, Joseph 57
Horace 96
Huitoto Indians 102, 108, 109, 114
Huron Indians 120
Hydroxymethylanthraquinone 72

Ideoblasts 26
Incense 62, 63, 64
India rubber tree 27, 36, 60
Inga Indians 74
Ink 91
Insects
  bark-boring 162, 163
  predatory 26, 63, 71, 163
Ira 74
Iroquois Indians 118

Jagua Indians 77
Jarawara Indians 74, 75
Jatobá 33
Jefferson, Thomas 97
Jeusebii, Caesariensis 117
Jesuits' bark 73
Jivaro Indians 105
Jonote colorado 105

Kapok 48, 167
Katydid 143
Kihei 105
Knot 32, 34
Kofán Indians 74, 75

Lacquers 62, 63, 64
Lamb, F. Bruce 80
Lapps 124
Larch 118
  western 48
Latex 13, 33, 55–61
Lactifers 24, 26
Laurel family 86
Lauro piraracu 33
Leather 90–95
Ledger, Charles 73
Legume family 63
Lemon 15
Lenticels 24, 27, 28
Lichens 45, 58, 148, 150, 151, 152, 153, 155
  bark 148, 149
  corticolous 148
  crustose 149
  foliicolous 148
  foliose 149
Linnaeus, Carolus 73
Linoleum 98
Liverworts 153
Lizards 143
London plane tree 23

MacIntosh, Charles 56
Mackenzie, Sir Alexander 117

Macucu
  chiador 33
  sangue 33
Magellan, Ferdinand 105, 119
Mahogany family 74
Maku Indians 75
Malaria 72, 73
Malecite Indians 117, 118
Mamaki 104
Manatee, Amazon 75
Manaus 57
Mangrove 92
  red 93
Manna gum tree 61
Maple 32, 118, 123
  coral bark 125
  paperbark 125
  red 125
  sugar 26, 149, 162
Marco Polo 104
Marmoset 136
Marquette, Pere Jacques 117
Mastic 64
Mata mata preto 33
Mavi 86, 89
McPhee, John 117
Menomini Indians 72
Meristem 24
Mestre 80
Metcalfe, C. R. 91

Mexican shaving brush 45
Micmac Indians 118
Milkweed 56
Mineral oils 56
Mojo Indians 104
Monardes 85
Montagnae Indians 119, 122, 131
Moonseed family 74
Morc Indians 104
Mosquito 106
Mosses 149, 156
Moths
  peppered 135
  scribbly gum 162
  tiger 138
  underwing 135
Mucilages 26
Muinto 105
Mulatta tree 33
Mulberry, paper 104, 105, 115
Mulch 14, 125
Munguba 111
Mura Indians 119
Myrrh 62, 63
Myrtle family 19

Nahuales 105
Naked Indian 39
Neem 52
Nettle family 104
Newfoundland 117

New York Botanical Garden 91
N, N—dimethyltryptamine 79, 80
Noradrenaline 125
Nut, alligator 33
  hazel 72
  myrobalan 91
  sapucaia 24
Nutmeg family 78
Nylander, W. 149

Oak 32, 90, 92
  Aleppo 91
  black 92
  California tanbark 92
  chestnut 92
  cork 24, 47, 96, 99, 101
  eastern 97
  red 92
  white 92, 149
Oaks 92
Oils 26, 31
Ojibway Indians 118, 120, 128
Oleoresins 64
Oliveira, Father Fernando 97
Orchids 154, 155

Palm
  royal 150
Palo verde 39
Particle board 125
Passamoquoddy Indians 119
Patagonia 119
Pa'u 105
Paumari Indians 79
Penobscot Indians 118
Pequiá 75
Periderm 24, 26, 39
Peterson, Bejer 163
Phellem 24, 25
Phloem 24, 25, 26, 33, 79, 85
  fibers 24
  secondary 24
Photosynthesis 26, 38–46
Pigaletta, Antonio 105
Pine
  Amboiana 16, 66
  Canary Island 30
  jack 149
  lacebark 125
  pitch 149
  ponderosa 48, 149
  red 48
  scotch 163
Pinene 64
Pines 63
Pliny the Elder 96
Polyphenols 91
Poplar 98
Potawatomi Indians 72
Priestly, Joseph 56

Punta Arenas 119

Quebracho 92
Queensland bottle tree 39
Quinine 72

Raleigh, Walter 74
Ramie 26
Redwood 47, 48
Resin 26, 33, 62–69, 78, 81, 118
Rhytidome 24, 25, 39
Ring-barking 26
Rittenorder of Knights 63
Royal Botanic Gardens, Kew 57
Rosin 64
Rotenone 75
Rubber 33, 55, 56, 57, 58, 59
  tree 54, 56, 58

Sachimanga 158
Safrole 85, 86
Saman 21, 69
Sandbox tree 48
Sanema Indians 79
Sapodilla family 57
Saponins 126
Sassafras 85
Savannas 48, 49
Schiaparelli, C. 90
Schultes, R. E. 79
Scolytids 163
Scribbly gum 162, 165
Sequoia, giant 48
Shellac 62
Sieve tubes 24, 25, 26
Silk cotton tree 44, 48, 53, 153, 159
Silk tree 42, 43
Silva, Milton da 33
Sioua Indians 74
Smith, Erla 125
Smith, John 98
Snails 170
Snuff 79
Soapbox tree 126
Sorva 57
Spines 48, 51, 52, 53
Spruce, Richard 55
Spruce 117, 163
  black 118
  white 118
Squirrel 136
Starch 26
Stinky toe 63, 119
Stilt roots 31
Stomata 24
Strawberry tree 44, 125, 127
Stridulation 164
Stringybark tree 130
Strychnine 74
Suberin 24

Suffrutices 48
Sumac 149
  family 64
Suya Indians 119

Talbor, Robert 73
Tanekaha 92
Tanning 90, 91
Tannins 14, 26, 90–95
  condensed 91
  hydrolyzable 91
Tapa 104, 105, 106
Tepees 129
Termites 164, 168, 169, 170
Terpenoids 56
Tetes de Boule Indians 118
Theophrastus 96
Thoreau, Henry David 117
Tierra del Fuego 119
Tikuna Indians 105
Treefrog, gray 162
Trumpet tree 151
Tryptamines 79, 80
Turmeric 104
Turpentine 64
Turtle, giant 75

Uasca 80
Ucuuba 78
Upas tree 76, 115

Vaillancourt, Henri 117
Varnishes 63, 64
Varro 96
Vascular cambium 24, 25
Vessels 26

Walnut, white 125
Walton, Frederick 98
Wardian case 57, 61
Wattle, African 92
  Australian 92
West, Ranyard 74
Wickham, Alexander 57
Willow, 92, 98
Witch hazel 72
Wizard of the Upper Amazon 80
Woodpeckers
  sapsucker 135

Yahgan Indians 119
Yanomami Indians 78, 79, 81, 82
Yew 73
Yoco vine 74, 75
Yohimbine 125, 126
Yuracare Indians 104

Zumarraya, Fray Juan de 105

174